PACIFIC NORTHWEST
LEGENDS & LORE

PACIFIC NORTHWEST
LEGENDS & LORE

IRA WESLEY KITMACHER

Illustrations by Jason McLean

THE
History
PRESS

Published by The History Press
Charleston, SC
www.historypress.com

Copyright © 2024 by Ira Wesley Kitmacher
All rights reserved

Front cover illustrations courtesy of Jason McLean.
Back cover: Pacific Northwest forest and river. *Courtesy of Pixabay, Foundry.*

First published 2024

Manufactured in the United States

ISBN 9781467157834

Library of Congress Control Number: 2024942215

I dedicate this book to my beloved family.

A special thank-you to my wife, Wendy, whose assistance and support were instrumental.

—*Ira Wesley Kitmacher*

CONTENTS

PART I. INTRODUCTION
1. Why I Wrote This Book—Pacific Northwest—Oregon
   and Washington 13
2. My Beliefs and Approach 19
3. Investigating and Fact-Finding 26

PART II. PACIFIC NORTHWEST LEGENDS AND LORE
1. Cryptids...31
2. Monsters..36
3. "We Don't Know a Millionth of One Percent
   About Anything" 38
4. Horror as a Reflection of Society and the Pacific Northwest 42
5. Pacific Northwest Cryptids 44
   Ape-like Creatures: Bigfoot and Agropelter.................................44
   Bear-like Creatures: Gumberoo and Bax 53
   Bird-like Creatures: Thunderbirds and the "Crooked Beak
   of Heaven" 57
   Cat-like Creatures: Ball-Tailed Cat, Klickitat Ape Cat
   and the "Twins" 63
   Dog-like Creatures: Werewolves and Dogman.............................68

Other Native Legends: Demons, Wendigo and Skinwalkers 75
Sea Serpents and Marine Creatures: Colossal Claude,
    Caddy the Cadborosaurus and the Devil's Lake Monster.............84
Vampiric Creatures: Vampires, Batsquatch and Chupacabra 91
6. Legendary Curses...98
    Curses and Protections Against Them..98
    Andelana and Streetcar Disasters 100
    Artesian Wells 102
    Bellingham Curse 103
    Cape Disappointment..104
    Chief Seattle's Curse 106
    Earthquakes, Tsunamis, Fires and Volcanoes 107
    Jake Bird Hex..109
    Lewis and Clark's Challenges, the Mystery of Meriwether Lewis
        and Sacagawea..110
    Maltby's Thirteen Steps to Hell 116
    Marcus Whitman 117
    Native Death Culture..118
    Nautical Superstitions 119
    Oakville Blobs 122
    Old Man of the Lake and the Spirits of Wizard Island.................122
    Oregon's Central Coast..123
    Pacific County Representatives 125
    Seattle Windshield Pitting Delusion...125
    Slavery...126
    Terrible Tilly Lighthouse..127
7. Lore 130
    Folklore, Superstitions and Urban Legends 130
        Bandage Man..136
        Billy Gohl..138
        Black-Eyed Children 140
        Cat Serial Killer..140
        Chinatowns 141

Contents

Columbia River Gorge 143

D.B. Cooper 144

Dead Zone 146

First Flying Saucer 148

Forest Man 150

Fort Stevens 151

Grandpa 152

Graveyard of the Pacific 152

Green River Killer 155

Mosquito Fleet 156

Old Hotel Olympian 157

Olympia Saved by Beer 157

Oregon Trail 158

Oregon Vortex, Gravity Hill and Other Oddities 162

Pirates 163

Satanic Sheriff 166

Severed Feet 166

Shanghaiing and Bunko Kelly 167

Ted Bundy 170

Tumwater State Bank 170

Victorian-Era Death Practices 171

Conclusion 175

Bibliography 179

About the Author 189

PART I
INTRODUCTION

1

WHY I WROTE THIS BOOK—
PACIFIC NORTHWEST—OREGON
AND WASHINGTON

From the beginning of time, people living in and visiting the Pacific Northwest (when I say Pacific Northwest, I'm talking about Oregon and Washington specifically) have told stories and tales of mysterious cryptids—"imaginary creatures"—legendary curses and folklore. These stories were often a mix of truth, exaggeration, fear, humor and wishful thinking. The more interesting of these stories took on lives of their own and were passed from one generation to the next. These are not my stories but rather tales I discovered, researched and am chronicling that have been passed by word of mouth and other means for decades, if not centuries. Hopefully I am shedding new light, garnering fresh insights and offering unique interpretations of these tales. I can't, in some cases, corroborate the complete accuracy of these stories but believe they round out the fascinating history of the Pacific Northwest.

Sometimes these folkloric tales continued in their original form, and other times they were embellished or altered. Some stories captured the public's attention by being reported on by newspapers and other media and serving as the focus of investigations, university studies, books, television programs and movies. These stories have been told in America by European pioneers and settlers, Natives, homegrown citizens and people from every corner of the globe. As a resident of the Pacific Northwest, I'm fascinated by its history, cryptids, legends and folklore—including hauntings, monsters, why something is the way it is and explanations for the otherwise unexplainable.

Shipwreck rescue, 1909. *Courtesy of Library of Congress.*

This is the fourth published book I have written that ties in with this genre. I briefly describe the prior three here. In addition to legends and lore, the other substantive area of "dark stories" told in the Pacific Northwest involve ghosts. I don't focus on hauntings in this book but do in three of my other books: *Haunted Graveyard of the Pacific*, *Spirits Along the Columbia River* and *Haunted Puget Sound*.

In my first published book, *Haunted Graveyard of the Pacific* (2021), I focused on hauntings at the mouth of the Columbia River, where the river meets the Pacific Ocean. Some believe the phrase "Graveyard of the Pacific" applies only to the confluence of the Pacific Ocean and the Columbia River. In fact, the Graveyard stretches along the Pacific Northwest coast, from Tillamook Bay in Oregon, past the treacherous Columbia Bar—the world's most dangerous entrance to a commercial waterway, near Astoria, Oregon—up the Washington coast to the Juan de Fuca Strait separating Canada from the United States and the western coast of Vancouver Island. Further, the Graveyard includes the waterways and the coasts that hug those waters. Over two thousand ships and countless lives have been lost to the Graveyard of the Pacific. I designed and led tours, based on the book, on an old-fashioned trolley of Washington's Long Beach Peninsula along the Graveyard of the Pacific. This book proved successful: it was named a "recommended read" by several magazines, and my publisher, Arcadia Publishing, adapted it into a children's book, *The Ghostly Tales of the Pacific Northwest* (2022).

In my second published book on Pacific Northwest ghost stories, *Spirits Along the Columbia River* (2022), I focused on the second-largest river after the Mississippi by volume in the United States, which unites all parts of the Pacific Northwest. Historically, the river garnered much interest on the part of explorers of many nations, including Spain, Great Britain and the United States. These countries struggled over possession of the river as they sought the legendary but imaginary Northwest Passage across the North American continent. The Northwest Passage through the Arctic was discovered in 1903 by Norwegian explorer Roald Amundsen. Their hope, unfulfilled, was to find a direct water route to the Pacific Ocean from the Mississippi River. This is what led to President Thomas Jefferson commissioning the 1804–6 Lewis and Clark expedition, the Corps of Discovery. This competition between nations, as well as the settling of the region, led to much pathos, conflict, opportunity and achievement. Frontiersmen, adventurers, soldiers, boatmen, early settlers, Natives and others suffered tragedies and death, resulting in numerous haunted tales.

In my third published book on area history and folklore, titled *Haunted Puget Sound* (2024), I focused on Washington's Puget Sound area, which is an inlet of the Pacific Ocean and interconnected waterways and basins connected to the Pacific and the coastal areas that bound them. It extends from the city of Olympia in the south to the colorfully named Deception Pass in the northern part of the Sound, with the cities of Tacoma, Seattle, Everett, Bellingham and others in between. Puget Sound is the second-largest estuary—a partially enclosed coastal body of salt-fresh mixed or brackish water—in the United States, after Chesapeake Bay in Maryland and Virginia. I designed and led nautical tours of Puget Sound on board an old-fashioned schooner and history and haunted folklore walking tours of Washington's capital, Olympia. Arcadia Publishing is adapting this book into a children's book, *The Ghostly Tales of Puget Sound* (2024).

In this, my fourth published book on the area, I focus on Pacific Northwest legends and lore.

The Pacific Northwest was one of the last parts of the United States to be explored and settled, making it seem more "wild" than other parts of the country. There is no better way to discover the beauty and history of the Pacific Northwest than to explore the cities, towns and waterways of the area, their history and the folklore. It is known for great hiking, boating, camping, fishing, biking, clamming, golfing, cranberry cultivation, oyster farming and tourism, while state parks with nineteenth-century military forts and national historic sites welcome history enthusiasts. Bald eagles, black bears, elk, deer and other wildlife call the area home. Killer whales or orca, humpback whales, dolphins, fish and other sea creatures live in

Pacific Northwest woods. *Courtesy of Pixabay, Foundry.*

the area's waters. While it offers breathtaking scenery, it has also been identified as an area of many dark legends and lore.

Natives have called this area home for at least ten thousand years, while White settlers are more recent inhabitants. The Spanish were the first Europeans to explore the area, beginning in 1774 with Juan Pérez, who sailed the Northwest coast; however, their efforts were more about defense against other European powers than establishing long-term settlements. Between 1791 and 1795, British Royal Navy captain George Vancouver explored the western regions of the North American Pacific coast on behalf of the Crown, including what would become Alaska, British Columbia, Hawaii, Oregon and Washington. The British constituted the primary non-Native population of the region until 1846, when Great Britain and the United States divided their respective parts of the Pacific Northwest at the forty-ninth parallel, creating America's Oregon Territory—the separate Washington Territory was created in 1853. Oregon was made a state in 1859, and Washington followed thirty years later in 1889.

In addition to the stories of individuals, there are other reasons supernatural tales and folklore abound in the Pacific Northwest. The geography, climate and natural disasters—fires, towering trees, rainforests, mountains, volcanoes, icy waters, earthquakes and tsunamis—are part of a long record of natural and man-made events that were not easy for Natives and others to make sense of without some supernatural explanation. Natives have long-standing beliefs in Bigfoot or Sasquatch, sea monsters, Thunderbirds, werewolves and other cryptids that help explain the unexplainable. The wildness of the region, as the last portion of the continental United States to be settled, influences such supernatural tales. There is also a strong Scandinavian influence in this area, bringing with it an abundance of supernatural folklore and tales.

The dark skies, high winds and thick fog that frequent this part of America round out the atmosphere of mystery and dread. So, if you see someone or something that appears strange and out of place, check again—it might be a cryptid or some other supernatural being.

My second published book, unrelated to the American Pacific Northwest, was *Monsters and Miracles: Horror, Heroes and the Holocaust* (June 2022). That book is centered on a very different world than America: it occurs primarily in the Nazi-occupied Europe of World War II. In that book, I wrote about my father, Al Kitmacher, a Holocaust survivor who led his family to temporary safety and through miracles survived the Warsaw ghetto and Nazi death camps, and my mother, Pearl Harris, a World War II

U.S. Navy veteran, who through her military service helped those suffering at the hands of the Nazis. I interwove their stories with World War II and Holocaust history, legends and lore. This included the Nazis' and their victims' underlying folklore—the Nazis believed they were descended from werewolves, and their enemies were vampires. It also explores horror, hero and superhero stories—who knew Captain America, Superman and others were created to persuade Americans to enter the war against the Nazis?!—beliefs in monsters, angels and the supernatural. I developed and will be co-leading with a European tour company an eleven-day tour of Poland and Germany based on that book.

2

MY BELIEFS AND APPROACH

T hose who believe in cryptids, legendary curses and lore say unexplainable forces influence everyday events. They say science and natural-law explanations don't shed light or explain the whole story. Though I would not describe myself as a "full believer" in these stories, I find them fascinating and would like to believe that some, or at least part, of the legends and lore are true. I also believe there are historical and societal reasons why these tales arose and exist, which I'll explain.

There are several reasons why I'm fascinated by American history, mysterious folklore and strange creatures. I was born and grew up in Massachusetts' Berkshire Hills on the border with New York State. Massachusetts was one of the first and most important areas of America to be settled by European immigrants. It is full of history, including Plymouth Rock, where the Pilgrims disembarked from the *Mayflower* in 1620, and America's first Thanksgiving, where colonists and Natives celebrated their thanks for a bountiful harvest in 1621. The Bay State—one of its nicknames—played a key leadership role in the Revolutionary War and independence from Great Britain and is where great Patriots like John Adams and Paul Revere were born. I take great pride in these historical events. Massachusetts was also home to one of the more mysterious and dark periods of American history, which fascinates me—the Salem Witch Trials of 1692 and 1693. That was the ultimate example of humans' preoccupation and fear of the supernatural and unknown, which led them to act in unfathomable ways toward their neighbors. I also lived in the

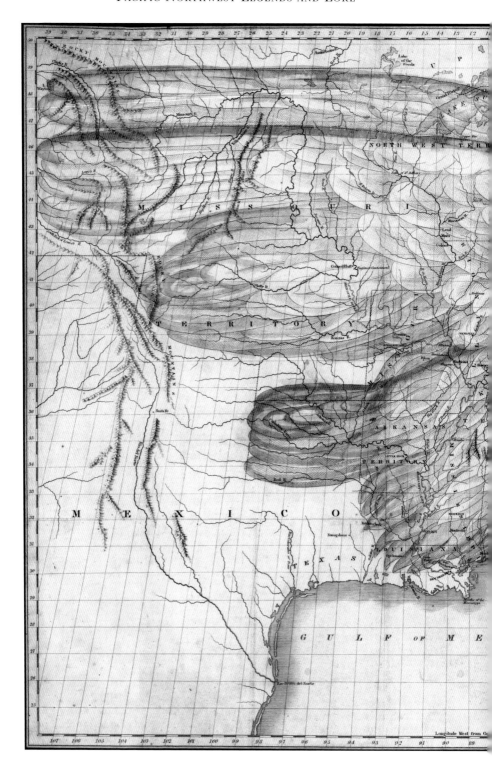

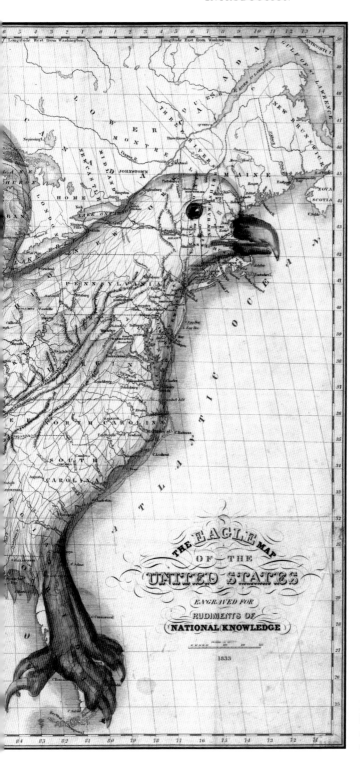

Eagle map of United States, 1833. *Courtesy of Library of Congress, Carey & Hart.*

Washington, D.C. area, whose history and museums I greatly appreciated in addition to being able to see the role that government plays in our everyday lives. In fact, my pride in being an American led me to spend my professional career working for the federal government. I've traveled extensively through and explored historic areas, including Gettysburg, Pennsylvania, and Williamsburg, Virginia. These experiences have deepened my love of history and the mysterious folklore that accompanies it. I've also lived in the Southwest and western United States, where I learned the importance of the Old West, ghost towns, nautical history and America's sense of manifest destiny, pushing for expanding the country—at times and unfortunately at the expense of others, including Natives. Each part of America has a fascinating history and accompanying mysterious and scary tales to tell.

My background is an eclectic one that, while on the surface might not appear to be tied directly to the subjects I write about, prepared me for this work. I retired from the U.S. government in 2019 after thirty-six years as a senior executive and manager and in other roles in the western United States and Washington, D.C. I am also a consultant, legal expert witness and licensed attorney. From the early 1980s to the mid-2000s, while based in the San Francisco Bay area, I made numerous trips throughout the Pacific Northwest to teach government leadership courses. It was during that time that I became fascinated by the region's atmosphere and history.

My wife, Wendy, and I moved from the West to Washington, D.C., for my work. My last role was that of chief human capital officer—human resources director for a federal agency. I was named that agency's senior executive of the year for 2019. After living in the D.C. area for thirteen years, we retired and decided to move back west. Our focus quickly centered on the Pacific Northwest. Our reasoning was based on the climate, history and beauty of the area. Upon retiring, I quickly found I had no desire to *fully* retire; I had to do something more, something worthwhile that would reflect my desire to acclimate to my new home and have a positive effect. To paraphrase American stateman Benjamin Franklin, if one wishes to be remembered, they should either write something worth reading or do something worth writing about. I chose the former!

I have served as a college and university professor teaching graduate and undergraduate courses at Georgetown University in Washington, D.C.; Portland State University in Oregon; Grays Harbor College in Aberdeen, Washington; Clatsop Community College in Astoria, Oregon; and Western Nevada College in Fallon. I developed a course on the haunted history

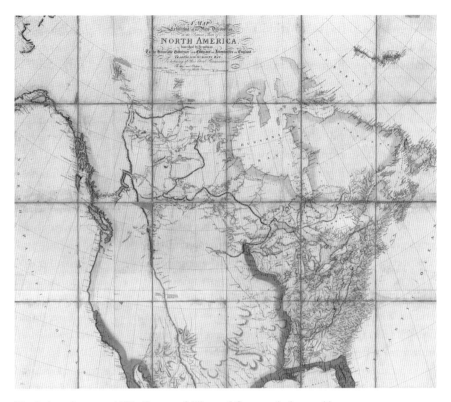

North America map, 1802. *Courtesy of Library of Congress, A. Arrowsmith.*

and folklore of the Pacific Northwest that I taught at Clatsop Community College. I have been featured in television news programs, documentaries and newspapers; on radio programs; at museums and conferences; in bookstores; and at other events where I have spoken about the history and folklore of the Pacific Northwest. I am an onboard historian and destination speaker for a major cruise ship line, focusing on waterways and coastal areas of the Pacific Northwest, New England and other parts of the United States. I am also a commissioner on a Pacific Northwest historic commission and a member of the Historical Writers' Association.

I have traveled extensively within the United States and in Europe, Canada and Mexico. Whenever I have a chance while traveling, I participate in ghost tours and other activities that focus on an area's history and haunted folklore. I have done this in the United States in many places, among them Charleston, South Carolina; Gettysburg, Pennsylvania; New Orleans, Louisiana; Salem, Massachusetts; San Francisco, California; Seattle, Washington; Sleepy Hollow, New York; Tombstone,

Statue of a monster. *Courtesy of Pixabay, Desertrose7.*

Arizona; and Williamsburg, Virginia. In Canada, I have visited Halifax, Montreal, Toronto, Victoria and Vancouver. In Europe, I have traveled through Austria, Belgium, France, Italy, Germany, Greece, Hungary, the Netherlands, Switzerland and the United Kingdom.

Growing up, my favorite books to read and movies to watch were those about the classic monsters, including Dracula, Frankenstein, the Creature from the Black Lagoon, the Headless Horseman of Washington Irving's 1820 "Legend of Sleepy Hollow," the Wolf Man and others. I have a particular affinity for two Abbott and Costello movies: 1946's *The Time of Their Lives* (involving Revolutionary War ghosts) and 1948's *Abbott and Costello Meet Frankenstein* (in which my favorite comedy team faces off against

Research materials. *Courtesy of Pixabay, ilovechile-travel.*

many of the classic monsters). I enjoyed reading about "inexplicable" and paranormal events—a person instantaneously combusting!—and books, such as *Ripley's Believe It or Not* and *Chariots of the Gods* about the weird and mysterious. In undergraduate school, my favorite courses were about Greek and Roman mythology and classic ghost stories, although my major was human resources management. Maybe these interests were a precursor to writing books like this one.

I have written this book to explore the Pacific Northwest's reported strange creatures, legendary curses and lore. I view my role as multifaceted: historian, investigator, interested tale teller, proud resident and tour guide. It is through these lenses that I wrote this book. As humans, we have particularly short memories; few remember tragedies that happened decades, let alone a century, ago. For example, other than the *Titanic* and a few notable others, we have virtually no memory of long-ago shipwrecks that resulted in multiple deaths. These disasters were all too common in the days before satellite navigation, GPS, cellphones and other safety measures. One of my primary reasons for writing books like this is to try to help preserve historical stories that might be lost over time.

3
INVESTIGATING AND FACT-FINDING

Using an evidence-based, investigatory approach to research and analyze reported supernatural phenomena, I found a wealth of information on the region's stories of cryptids, legendary curses and lore. Sources include Native oral history, settler and adventurer accounts and books, newspapers from the mid-1800s to present day, recorded stories, government records and social media. I have not included legends or stories that lack evidence, and I have taken great pains to include, in the bibliography, all the source materials I reviewed and that informed my writing, and/or I found of interest, making sure to give credit where credit is due and offer additional resources.

It is my nature to question whether these tales are based on fact and logic. I pride myself on my careful research, which I have practiced over the last forty years while wearing many different professional hats. But in researching these tales, it is clear not everything can be proven beyond a reasonable doubt.

In conducting investigations and fact-finding, there are different types of evidence to be reviewed and methods to collect them, including the following:

REAL EVIDENCE consists of those items that were present and played a role in the story or legend, including evidence that can be touched, smelled, seen or in some other way sensed.

DOCUMENTARY EVIDENCE, which documents the events in question, including government reports, newspaper accounts, university studies, the Bible, logs and others.

DEMONSTRATIVE EVIDENCE includes animations, drawings, diagrams and maps.

TESTIMONIAL EVIDENCE consists of witness statements, interviews with those who observed or experienced the events and oral history.

DIGITAL EVIDENCE emanates from media and technology, including movies, documentaries, social media, blogs, emails, telephone calls and others.

SITE VISITS to the locations, buildings and physical source of the legend or story are very helpful.

In a book like this, there are bound to be overlaps and similarities between legends. This is in part because tales tend to emerge from similar circumstances—dark forests, salty seas, insurmountable mountains and the like—with similar evidence such as large, hairy ape-like beasts, serpentine sea creatures and so on. I am sensitive to readers finding repetitive information and have tried to include examples that are unique.

Finally, I chose the stories to discuss based on five factors:

1. The length of time—how old a tale—has been told.
2. How widely spread—frequency and/or prevalence—the telling of the story appears to be.
3. Greatest impact on the surrounding community.
4. The sources and amount of proof or evidence that exists about the story.
5. Stories I find interesting after reviewing hundreds, if not thousands, thinking that if they're interesting to me, they may be interesting to others.

Please join me as we journey through the Pacific Northwest in search of cryptids, legendary curses and lore. I hope you enjoy reading this book as much as I enjoyed writing it. I strongly encourage you to explore the area and visit—of course following all applicable rules and laws, respecting privacy, hours of operation, etc.—the many businesses and landmarks that are open to the public that we'll discuss.

PART II
PACIFIC NORTHWEST LEGENDS AND LORE

1

CRYPTIDS

In this first section, in talking about Pacific Northwest legends and lore, we focus on cryptids. The term *cryptozoology* was first used in a 1955 book by Belgian French scientist, explorer, researcher and writer Bernard Heuvelmans, considered the "father of cryptozoology." Cryptozoologist J.E. Wall first used the term *cryptid* in the summer 1983 issue of the International Society of Cryptozoology newsletter to replace a "sensational" term like *monster*. There are fine distinctions between cryptids, mythological creatures and monsters, and I at times use the terms interchangeably.

Cryptids are presumably imaginary creatures, sometimes with supernatural qualities, whose existence is considered empirically—based on observation or experience—lacking by science. However, they are believed to be real by some based on available evidence, stories and/or personal observation and experience. While seemingly hundreds of different types of cryptids have been reported all over the world, and many in every U.S. state, there is a concentration of almost forty different creatures, with thousands of sightings in the Pacific Northwest. A long-standing and the best-known example of a Pacific Northwest cryptid is Bigfoot, which, although still not proven by science to exist, is believed by many to be real.

Mythological creatures are like cryptids and are often found in religion and classic Egyptian, Greek, Native American, Roman or other mythologies; an example is the Greek flying horse Pegasus.

Finally, monsters are, again, like cryptids that are considered abnormal, unnatural and often dangerous. An example of a monster is the blood-

Mythological creature, 2024. *Courtesy of Jason McLean.*

sucking vampire. As there are overlaps between some cryptids and monsters, I list a few in both categories.

Cryptids, mythological creatures and monsters have fascinated people for as long as can be remembered and have been featured in a wide variety of books, television programs, movies, podcasts, magazines, newspapers and other media. These stories were told in ancient times and continue today. Whether the vampire Dracula, the mighty gorilla King Kong, the man-made Frankenstein monster, the Wolf Man or the giant vengeful shark in *Jaws*, these creatures—and there are many, many more—figure prominently in our society.

Cryptozoology is a pseudoscience, with findings and explanations not in compliance with traditional science, that seeks to prove the existence of these supernatural folkloric creatures. Cryptozoologists refer to the creatures they seek to prove exist as cryptids, and in addition to Bigfoot, there are sea serpents, the Thunderbird and others.

The Pacific Northwest's supernatural creatures, again close to forty, described in this book include but are not limited to:

APE-LIKE CREATURES. Bigfoot is the best known of these, and the greatest number of Bigfoot sightings are in Washington, closely followed by Oregon. They are also reported in every other state. The creature is portrayed as large with huge feet, standing between seven and ten feet tall. Other creatures are smaller, resemble apes of varying types and are said to inhabit forests and mountain ranges. Folklore originated in Native and European cultures, and sightings continue.

BEAR-LIKE CREATURES. Including the Gumberoo and other bear-like cryptids, these are said to resemble bears we are familiar with such as the black bear, the polar bear and so on, but with supernatural qualities.

BIRD-LIKE CREATURES. These include blackbirds, eagles and the Thunderbird, which is said to possess supernatural power and strength sufficient to cause thunder—hence the name—when it flaps its wings.

CAT-LIKE CREATURES. Including Washington's Klickitat Ape Cat, these resemble cats but are very large, have supernatural powers and don't fit into any known cat species.

DOG-LIKE CREATURES. The werewolf is the best known of these cryptids, a humanoid creature with canine features that transforms from people due to being bitten by a werewolf, a magic spell or some other reason. Also, there are other creatures that in some ways resemble dogs.

OTHER NATIVE LEGENDS. This category includes tricksters, shape-shifters, cannibals and other cryptids that helped Natives explain the otherwise unexplainable.

Bigfoot, 2024. *Courtesy of Jason McLean.*

Sea Serpents and Marine Creatures. Legendary snake, dragon and dinosaur-like creatures are said to inhabit the oceans and rivers, including Oregon and Washington's Columbia River, the Pacific coast region known as the Graveyard of the Pacific, Washington's Puget Sound and others, and are described in various cultures' mythologies.

Vampire-like Cryptids. These include Batsquatch and others, some of which are said to feed on the blood of the living.

2
MONSTERS

The Latin word for monsters is *monstrum*, meaning "ominous" or "warning signs." Monsters are often reflective of cultural fears. Because they live at the edges of what we believe is possible, monsters seem to always manage to get away when we hunt them and then return to haunt or prey on us. Like with cryptids, there are many different types reported in the Pacific Northwest.

As shown in books, movies and television programs, some cryptids and monsters are said to be undead, often portrayed as evil, vengeful creatures that prey on the living. These man-made or naturally occurring supernatural creatures, many of which are found in the Pacific Northwest, are said to take on various forms:

BOOGEYMEN: Potentially dangerous creatures that resemble men but are imbued with strange supernatural attributes or powers. A Pacific Northwest example of a boogeyman is Bandage Man of Cannon Beach, Oregon, discussed later.

DEMONS: Evil entities that trick and make deals with people in exchange for their souls. Many Pacific Natives' folklore discusses these evil creatures and entities.

MUMMIES: Intentionally preserved animated corpses. Bandage Man, again, could be seen as a Pacific Northwest mummy.

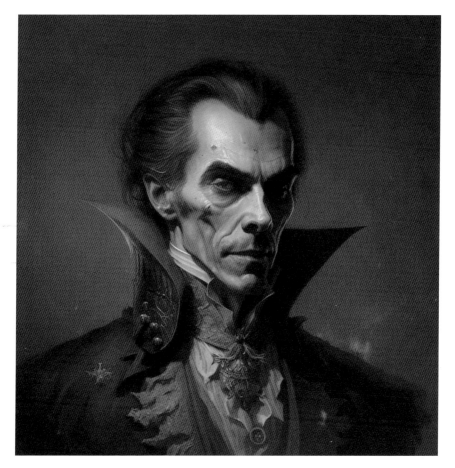

Vampire. *Courtesy of Pixabay, JulieZimmi2.*

SHAPE-SHIFTERS: Entities, sometimes humanoid, with the ability to physically transform themselves through superhuman ability, divine intervention, demonic manipulation, sorcery, spells or having inherited the ability. Many of the aforementioned Pacific Northwest cryptids—for example, dog-like or cat-like creatures—are also shape-shifters.

VAMPIRES: Undead creatures that feed on the blood of humans and other living beings. There are several Pacific Northwest vampiric creatures we'll discuss.

ZOMBIES: Reanimated corpses that feed on human flesh. Bandage Man, again, may fit this category of monster.

3

"WE DON'T KNOW A MILLIONTH OF ONE PERCENT ABOUT ANYTHING"

It is easier to dismiss claims of cryptids, legendary curses and lore than to prove their existence. In most cases, there simply is no rock-solid proof of the existence of these reported paranormal occurrences. However, I'm frequently reminded of Thomas Edison's statement about not knowing a millionth of one percent about anything. I fully believe what Edison— creator of the light bulb, phonograph and motion picture camera—said is true. We know far less about the world around us than what exists. Further, William J. Broad, in a 2005 *New York Times* article, noted that scientists argue so much of Earth remains unexplored, no doubt new surprises, including strange creatures, will show up. In his 2006 book *Singing Whales and Flying Squid: The Discovery of Marine Life*, author Richard Ellis said he was sure, given how big and deep the oceans are, unseen and unsolved mysteries await discovery. One needs to look no further than the world of cryptids to see that what was once dismissed as fanciful, inaccurate and possibly insane thinking in fact is true. The following ten "imaginary" creatures—once thought to exist only in folklore—do really exist:

Thomas Edison, 1911. *Courtesy of Library of Congress*.

BONDEGEZOU: Not as well-known as some of the other animals on this list, this Western Papua New Guinea tree-dwelling marsupial was first discovered in the 1980s by Australian scientist Tim Flannery. It has black and white fur, walks on two legs and resembles a tiny man.

GIANT AND COLOSSAL SQUID: These creatures—some of which are found in Washington's Puget Sound as well as the Pacific Ocean off the Pacific Northwest—seemingly arise from humans' nightmares about the kraken and Greek Scylla sea monsters and were first reported in 1857 and 1925, respectively. The colossal squid is larger, reaching a length of up to forty-six feet and weights exceeding 1,100 pounds. In 2004, Japanese researchers first took photos of the giant squid, and in 2006, they caught a live twenty-four-foot female. A specimen of a colossal squid, captured in 2007, is on display at the Museum of New Zealand Te Papa Tongarewa.

GORILLA: Although an expedition from the Phoenician merchant city of Carthage 2,500 years ago to the western coast of Africa discovered a group of wild gorillas, the animals were thought to be cryptids until the mid-nineteenth century. In 1847, American physician and missionary Thomas Staughton Savage and naturalist Jeffries Wyman found western gorilla bones in Liberia. Mountain gorillas—and silverback gorillas in particular—were not known to exist until 1902 and were considered cryptids.

KANGAROO: The kangaroo was considered an imaginary creature, said to resemble a giant, hopping mouse, until the late eighteenth century. It wasn't until 1770 that Sir Joseph Banks, on Captain Cook's exploration ship HMS *Endeavour*, first reported the existence of the animal in Australia.

KOMODO DRAGON. Until 1910, this creature—which can grow to ten feet long and up to 150 pounds in weight and has a fearsome reputation—was thought to be a myth. Lieutenant Steyn van Hensbroek of the Dutch Colonial Administration in Indonesia caught and killed a dragon on Komodo Island in Indonesia. Explorer W. Douglas Burden returned to New York City in 1926 with twelve preserved specimens and two live dragons. His expedition served as an inspiration for the 1933 movie *King Kong*.

OARFISH: A giant—up to fifty-six feet long—bony fish, usually found in the deep seas. Occasionally, the bodies of these creatures wash ashore and have given rise to legends of a variety of sea serpents. The first live oarfish was not filmed until 2001.

OKAPI: Was fancifully called the "African unicorn" through the nineteenth century. It was dismissed as a blend of zebra, donkey, deer and antelope. In 1890, British American explorer Sir Henry Morton Stanley first reported the animal. In 1901, British explorer Sir Harry Hamilton Johnston found an okapi skeleton and skin and sent them to the British Museum, classified as a new species. It is known as the "forest giraffe" and is the giraffe's only living relative.

PLATYPUS. This thought-to-be-imaginary creature and hoax, combining the duck, otter and beaver, was discovered by Europeans in 1798. Several expeditions in the late eighteenth century proved it to be real, and George Shaw, keeper of the British Museum's natural history collections, was the first to scientifically describe it, in 1799. It is a unique creature, one of only five living mammal species to lay eggs. The other four are anteaters— mammals were thought to give birth only to live young. Further, the platypus is venomous, again rare for mammals.

RHINOCEROS AND NARWHAL: Ancient Roman philosopher and historian Pliny the Elder (AD 24–79) wrote what some consider to be the first encyclopedia, *Naturalis Historia*, some two thousand years ago. In it, he makes mention of a horned animal with an elephant's feet, a boar's tail and a body like a large horse. He said the creature couldn't be captured alive. The rhino and the narwhal, a toothed—although it looks like a horn—whale from the freezing waters around Greenland and other locations, gave rise to stories of the mythical unicorn, the horse-like creature with a horn protruding from its forehead. Both the rhino and narwhal, originally thought to be cryptids, proved to be real animals. Relatives of the rhino date back 55–50 million years ago. When English explorer Martin Frobisher discovered the narwhal in 1577, he named it the "sea unicorn."

Similarly, when dinosaur fossils were first discovered in 1824, there were those—and there are still some—who just wouldn't believe creatures as large as dinosaurs existed. Not hard to understand when you remember nearly 65 million years passed between the time the last dinosaur walked the earth and people first appeared. Fascinating to think that the first president of the United States, George Washington, would likely have known nothing about dinosaurs—he died in 1799. Since that first fossil

Dinosaur skeleton, 1913. *Courtesy of Library of Congress, Harris & Ewing photographer.*

was found, scientists are in general agreement dinosaurs really existed. Interestingly, some people believed dinosaurs and other extinct animal bones were in fact those of the folkloric dragon—winged, scaly, fire-breathing reptiles. People in the Asian, European and other ancient worlds had a widespread belief in and fear of dragons.

4

HORROR AS A REFLECTION OF SOCIETY AND THE PACIFIC NORTHWEST

Horror stories, movies and shows, often with cryptids and monsters as the focus, are intended to elicit the core emotions of fear and terror. Often, they reflect anxieties of the time and/or warn of or predict anxieties to come. Horror stories have been described as stories or allegories that contain moral meaning in the guise of monsters and other supernatural beings. These stories are used to deliver a broader message about real-world issues. The core emotions horror stories evoke are fear and terror, and the overall plot arcs of horror stories tend to be similar: The protagonists—heroic main figures, who live a relatively simple existence—work to get by in their day-to-day lives. The antagonists—in the form of monsters and evil beings—attack and claim initial victory. Finally, the protagonists attempt to overcome evil.

In my 2022 book *Monsters and Miracles: Horror, Heroes and the Holocaust*, I refer to numerous horror stories and movies. The two earliest horror movies, and ones that reflected Germans' anxieties and fears around World War I and foretelling World War II are *The Golem* (1915) and *Nosferatu* (1922). Interestingly, a golem—a man-made creature intended to protect the people against persecution, is thought to be in part Mary Shelley's model for her Frankenstein's monster—misunderstood, villainized, ostracized and deemed less than human, like the Nazis' victims. Many of the other movies I reference were created in the 1930s and 1940s and reflect this anxiety. These include 1931's *Dracula*, based on Bram Stoker's 1897 novel, starring Hungarian Bela Lugosi as an ancient, bloodthirsty vampire; 1931's *Frankenstein*, based on Mary Shelley's 1818 novel, starring Boris Karloff, in which a scientist plays god by creating a living being from dead flesh; 1933's *The Invisible Man* starring Claude Rains, in which a secret experiment to become invisible goes awry; and 1941's *The Wolf Man* starring Lon Chaney Jr., about a man who is bitten by a werewolf and becomes one. Germans of the 1930s and 1940s—many well-educated and sophisticated—had a choice like the primary character in *Dr. Jekyll and Mr. Hyde*, between evil and good. They all too often followed the path of evil.

There are many chilling books, movies and television shows set in the Pacific Northwest, reflecting the numerous tales of paranormal phenomena found in this northwestern corner of America. These include the vampire and werewolf *Twilight* saga, the pirate treasure movie *The Goonies*, the TV series *Supernatural*—one of my favorites—the remake of *The Fog* and the drama-mystery *Twin Peaks*, all made or based in the Pacific Northwest and close by. Even *The Shining*, for which Oregon's Timberline Lodge served as the movie's Colorado-based Stanley Hotel for exterior shots, features a package of "Willapoint Minced Clams," sourced in the Graveyard of the Pacific at Willapa Bay, Washington.

Next, we'll move into discussing the Pacific Northwest's close to forty specific cryptids.

5

PACIFIC NORTHWEST CRYPTIDS

Ape-like Creatures: Bigfoot and Agropelter

Bigfoot may be the most famous cryptid in the world—with the Loch Ness Monster of Scotland, the Native legendary Skinwalker and others in competition. In 2022, the word *Bigfoot* was searched 4 million times in the United States on Google, the second-greatest number of searches for cryptids behind the Skinwalker—discussed under "Other Native Legends." Legends of Bigfoot—also called Sasquatch—meaning "wild men" in the Native Salish language, go back beyond recorded history. Similar legends exist in Australia, where they're called the Yowie, and Asia with the Yeti or Abominable Snowman and the Chinese Wildman with reddish hair. The primary difference between them and Bigfoot seems to be location. While Bigfoot is thought of as the quintessential Pacific Northwest cryptid—some describe the region as the Sasquatch capital of the world—it has been reported in every American state. In the American South, the creature is referred to as the Boggy Creek Monster, the Fouke Monster, the Jonesville Monster, the Skunk Ape and the Southern Sasquatch. In Arizona, the Mogollon Monster is a Bigfoot-like creature first seen in 1903 and described as large, with massive shoulders and chest, deep-set eyes, long white hair, matted beard, wearing no clothing, with talon-like claws at least two inches long. Appalachia is said to be home to as many as twelve different types of Bigfoot. In Ohio, there is the human-looking Grassman; elsewhere there is the former cave-dwelling and dangerous Midnight Whistler, and in West

Bigfoot, 2024. *Courtesy of Jason McLean.*

Virginia is the apple-eating Yahoo. The jet black–furred Wildman is said to be the most aggressive Bigfoot in Appalachia and was alleged to have killed seven Shawnee Natives in the 1700s. Maryland has the Sykesville Monster, which was seen in the 1970s and 1980s. Most of these creatures, like the Pacific Northwest Bigfoot, are described as shy, reclusive and intelligent, like most apes, and very large.

Pacific Northwest Natives strongly believed Sasquatch was real, and tales of his existence have been passed down through oral history over thousands of years. There are ancient stories of "peculiar creatures," "mountain devils" and "wild men" that lurked near villages and left immense footprints. Natives said one location the creatures frequented was Washington's Mount St. Helens. Members of the Plateau tribes, such as those at the Warm Springs Reservation in north-central Oregon, described Sasquatch as a "stick Indian," a potentially hostile being who stole salmon and confused people by whistling, causing them to become lost. Some Native legends described Bigfoot as a paranormal creature with the power to read people's minds. Other legends said Bigfoot used Chupacabras, discussed later along with vampiric creatures, almost like bloodhounds for hunting. As documented in 1865 by ethnographer George Gibbs, Pacific Northwest Natives described the Tsiatko, "hirsute and wild Indians" of the woods. Natives told tales of these large, wild and hairy men. In 1898, Chief Mischelle of the Nlaka'pamux shared the story of a creature he called "the benign-faced-one." Members of the Lummi tell tales of Ts'emekwes, while other tribes use different names, including Siet' ko, Stiyaha, Kwi-kwiyai and Skoocooms. Though most tales describe benign giants living among the people and stealing salmon from fishing nets, others feature dangerous, rock throwing and even cannibalistic creatures. According to a nineteenth-century Native legend, children were warned against saying the names of these creatures for fear the beings would hear them and carry off or kill someone. To this day, tales of these beings are still told on reservations.

The stories of Scandinavian immigrants—Finns in particular, who immigrated in great numbers to the Pacific Northwest in the nineteenth century—may have contributed to the Sasquatch legend. One mythical Finnish creature said to be found in the woods is called the Peikko. The Peikko is reported to be a slow, large, hairy, wild ape–like creature. Some are said to be aggressive, and they are thought to be related to trolls, giants and goblins. It could be that the legend of the Peikko, brought to America by immigrating Finns, added to Sasquatch sightings in the Pacific Northwest and elsewhere.

Bigfoot stories in colonial America started in about 1700, with the large, hairy, ape-like creatures of the forest screaming loudly and stealing livestock. There were also stories of shape-shifting creatures—a topic for later in the book—turning into Bigfoot, adding to the supernatural overtones of the being. I recount some of the stories about Bigfoot here.

Bigfoot began capturing the American public's attention when it was first widely described in Oregon in 1904. Sightings of these hairy wild men were reported by settlers in Oregon's Coastal Range mountains, with similar accounts spread by miners and hunters in later decades.

In 1924, gold prospectors and miners on Washington's Mount St. Helens claimed to have encountered giant "apes" in an incident that was widely reported in national and international newspapers. They were labeled in one report as "fabled beasts." Fred Beck, Gabe Lefever, John Peterson, Marion Smith and Smith's son Roy described "gorilla men." These creatures, not yet named Bigfoot, were covered in long black hair from head to foot and said to have gorilla faces, four-inch-long ears that stuck straight up and the ability to stand upright and walk like humans with four short and stubby toes on each gigantic foot. They were seven to nine feet tall, each weighing about four hundred pounds. One of the miners, Fed Beck, reported shooting one of the creatures with his rifle and watched it fall into the gorge. That night, the miners claimed the creatures attacked them, seemingly in retaliation for the earlier violence. The miners said they felt boulders striking the outside of their hunting cabin. Then they felt huge bodies slamming themselves against the cabin's walls and doors. Finally, the giant apes ripped a hole into the roof of the cabin, threw rocks and struck Beck, the shooter, knocking him unconscious for almost two hours. Sunrise seemed to cause the attacking apes to retreat, and the miners escaped into the woods. Upon hearing their story, the U.S. Forest Service investigated. Rangers J.H. Huffman and William Welch accompanied Beck back to the cabin but later said they found nothing to convince them of an attack. Years later, it was reported that an experienced skier disappeared from near the same location, fueling stories that the apes had again attacked a human. There was no proof of this, but the story persisted. Revisiting the site fifty years later, in 1974, a newspaper reporter wrote about tracks found in the area as well as additional witness sightings of large, hairy, mysterious creatures walking like men in the woods. The area is nicknamed "Ape Canyon" in remembrance of the purported 1924 incident.

Around 1958, loggers to the east and west of the Cascade Mountains in Oregon and Washington began reporting sightings of Sasquatch-like creatures and discovering their immense tracks along logging roads. Witnesses reported observing these beings crossing roads at night, striding furtively through forest and mountain terrain and digging for ground squirrels in rock piles to east. In 1958, the *Humbolt Times*, a small Northern California newspaper, reported a road construction crew discovered sixteen-inch-long humanlike footprints and labeled, for the first time, the creature creating the footprints "Bigfoot."

In 1967, Roger Patterson and Bob Gimlin were riding horses in the wooded Bluff Creek in Northern California. They said they came across a large apelike creature. As it attempted to flee, Patterson filmed it before it disappeared. The well-known, less-than-one-minute footage shows a large, ape-like hairy creature walking upright on two legs, looking back at the two men. Skeptics labeled the film a hoax, a man in a gorilla costume. No one has been able to prove or disprove the legitimacy of the film. Patterson died of cancer in 1972 and claimed the creature was real right up to his death. Gimlin continues to deny it was a hoax. Some scientists say it was a person in an ape suit, while others examining the film on computers say the creature's gait was nonhuman and no one could have created such a convincing, natural-looking apelike costume in 1967.

In 1970, Peter Byrne established the Bigfoot Information Center at The Dalles along Oregon's and Washington's Columbia River, featuring documented eyewitness testimony and footprints. In 1976, Byrne submitted a sample of what he said was Bigfoot hair and tissue to the FBI for testing. The FBI analyzed the samples "in the interest of research and scientific inquiry" and wrote, in a 1977 memo, that the samples came from a deer. Byrne continued to believe Bigfoot is real, noting a large footprint found in the Pacific Northwest from an upright mammal with each foot having five toes and the creature having a forty-six-inch stride—a six-foot-tall man's stride is typically thirty inches.

In 1994, a former U.S. Forest Service patrolman reported seeing an entire family of Bigfoot—there is some debate whether the plural of Bigfoot is Bigfoot, Bigfoots or Bigfeet, in the Blue Mountains of southeast Washington. He recorded video footage of the creatures, but it was shaky and grainy. His sighting is one of numerous Bigfoot sightings in Oregon and Washington state parks and other lands by people of virtually every age and occupation.

In 1995, the Bigfoot Researchers Organization (BFRO) was founded and says it's the only scientific research organization focusing on Bigfoot. They house and offer online documentaries, clips of purported Bigfoot sounds and a database of information.

In 2019, leading Bigfoot researcher Cliff Barackman opened the North American Bigfoot Center—a museum in Boring, Oregon.

In 2020, a Grants Pass, Oregon psychologist claimed to have heard, smelled and seen a Bigfoot while hiking over the Fourth of July weekend in Oregon Caves National Monument. He said he first smelled something like a skunk, but it was much stronger and worse. He said he heard the creature making "whoo, whoo" noises. The psychologist then said he saw a tall, dark, hairy creature peer out from behind a tree and stare at his family He described having been chased in Alaska some six years earlier by a grizzly bear and remarked that this was not a bear. The creature then wandered away. Despite doubters, the psychologist stuck by his story as real.

On January 22, 2020, a Washington State Department of Transportation (WSDOT) webcam captured photos of a Bigfoot-like creature walking through the snow on Sherman Pass near State Route 20. WSDOT posted the photos saying, "Sasquatch spotted!!!" Soon after, there was a separate Bigfoot sighting on Washington's Snoqualmie Pass wildlife overcrossing, a bridge built to make it easier for wildlife to cross safely over the highway. WSDOT's Snoqualmie Pass posted video footage of the creature and wrote, "I think Bigfoot is making the rounds across our mountain passes." Another Washington state agency with state and federal roles, the Washington Air National Guard's Western Air Defense Sector, headquartered at Joint Base Lewis-McChord between Olympia and Tacoma, Washington, which operates twenty-four hours a day, seven days a week monitoring 73 percent of the United States and Canada for risks from the air, has Bigfoot as its mascot. The sector's tagline or motto is, I'm paraphrasing, that like Bigfoot, they're rarely seen and heard but continuously observe and serve as a warning messenger. Related, in a U.S. Air Force survival training map of Washington, Bigfoot was listed as one of the dangerous creatures trainees might encounter, along with mountain lions, black bears and bobcats; it's not clear if this warning was tongue-in-cheek.

One British researcher in 2024 found Bigfoot sightings may be linked to the presence of black bears, which can be many colors other than black. The study found an average of 1 Bigfoot sighting for every 5,000 black bears, and as the number of bears goes up, so do Sasquatch sightings. The researcher's thought is that people may be misidentifying bears as Bigfoot. While there may be a correlation between bears and Bigfoot, it may also be that both are present in mountainous, forested areas. Interestingly, the study found there to be reported Bigfoot sightings in areas with relatively few black bears such as Florida, which has the third-highest number of Bigfoot sightings with 323 and about 4,000 black bears.

There have been many movies about Bigfoot, with the first arriving in 1970. Most of these portray Bigfoot as a dangerous creature, such as 1989's *Night of the Demon*, and 2014's *Exists*, while some are more comedic and portray Bigfoot as a benevolent, friendly creature like 1987's *Harry and the Hendersons*—one of my favorites—and 2019's animated *Missing Link*.

The percentage of adult Americans who believe Bigfoot is real increased from 11 percent in 2020 to 13 percent in 2022. Americans living in the West are more likely to believe, with 15 percent agreeing with the statement "Bigfoot/Sasquatch is a real, living creature." This compares with 11 percent of those living in the Northeast who agree with that statement. Those living in rural areas are more likely to believe this than those who live in cities and the suburbs. Younger people, thirty-five to fifty-four, are more likely to believe in Bigfoot than older Americans. At least two professors, from Idaho State and Washington State Universities, have indicated they believe Bigfoot, based on the evidence, may be real. Idaho State's website describes "The Bigfoot Mapping Project (BMP)," to communicate on technology used for Bigfoot field research. BMP displays a "heat map" of Bigfoot sightings in the Pacific Northwest and elsewhere and can be filtered according to date and time of sighting; whether footprints, vocalization or "wood knocks"—said to be how Bigfoot communicated with each other—were detected; gender; whether Bigfoot young were seen; and color. It also allows for submission of new sightings. It's fascinating!

There have been over twenty-three thousand Bigfoot sightings across the United States, with the greatest number, at least two thousand sightings, in Washington. The best chance of spotting the elusive creature may be in the Blue Mountains, Okanogan County, in northeastern Washington near the Canadian border. However, the nationwide lawncare company Lawn Love, which researched the topic, found several cities in Washington and Oregon, including Tacoma, Seattle and Portland at or near the top, to be hotbeds of Sasquatch sightings. I personally spoke with a Washington man in his fifties who swears he encountered a Bigfoot many years ago while camping with a friend. He said the creature appeared docile but still "scared him to death." They stared at each other for a period before the creature wandered off.

A love of and visiting the great outdoors seem to be correlated with the belief Bigfoot is real. Those who believe in Bigfoot are more likely—59 percent—to visit national and state parks several times a year. Seemingly confirming the existence of Bigfoot in the Pacific Northwest, a 1969, amended in 1984, Skamania County, Washington ordinance makes it illegal to kill the "endangered" ape-like creature, with a $1,000 fine and/one year in jail as the penalty. Similarly, Whatcom County, Washington, passed a resolution in 1992 proclaiming the county as a Sasquatch protection and refuge area, with a fine not to exceed $10,000 and/or up to five years in jail as the penalty for the felony of "any premeditated, willful and wanton slaying of any such creature." In 1970, Washington governor Dan Evans proclaimed the "Great Sasquatch" to be the state's official monster. Washington Senate Bill 5816 was introduced in 2018 to declare Bigfoot the state's official cryptid; however, it didn't make it past the introductory stage. Grays Harbor County on the Pacific coast in Washington has declared itself a Sasquatch protection and refuge area, and an annual Bigfoot conference called the Sasquatch Summit is held there. Researchers, academics, Native representatives and members of the public are invited to participate.

Bigfoot has permeated American culture—related souvenirs, tchotchkes and collectables playing off the legends are ubiquitous. One cannot enter a retail store in the Pacific Northwest and many other places in America without seeing them on display. There are hats, T-shirts, plush-stuffed toys, action figures, slippers in the shape of Bigfoot's feet and air fresheners. Yard signs for display include "Caution—Bigfoot Area," "Warning—Property Protected by Big Foot," "Warning—Please Do Not Feed the Sasquatch" and others. There have even been annual festivals, termed "Sasquatch Music," and other Sasquatch festivals held in George and Longview, Washington, and elsewhere.

Some believe Bigfoot is in fact a Gigantopithecus, a gigantic ape that stood ten feet tall, weighed up to 1,200 pounds and lived beside early humans for over 1 million years. The large ape-like creature crossed the Bering Land Bridge from Asia and settled in North America. Fortunately for humanity, this enormous ape's diet was almost exclusively bamboo. However, scientists believe the Gigantopithecus went extinct 100,000 years ago in the Pleistocene period. Those who believe Bigfoot exists dispute scientists' findings. It is thought that the existence of Bigfoot, like other "wild men," presents the question, "What might human beings be without civilization?" For some, Bigfoot is a symbol of the wild, untamed and related freedom of wandering in mountainous forests. However, some people have attempted to gain attention and become famous by falsely claiming to have seen these creatures.

Although Bigfoot are generally considered not dangerous, a fear of Bigfoot could be because of movie portrayals, Native and Finnish folklore, reported

Ape-like creatures, 2024. *Courtesy of Jason McLean.*

attacks such as the 1924 one on miners and a general fear of the unknown. A fear of Bigfoot has been termed Bigfootphobia, Sosantoglitaphobia (fear of Sasquatch) and megalophobia (fear of large things). There seems to be no way to protect yourself from a Bigfoot, other than avoiding them. Experts indicate bullets, pepper spray and other weapons have little effect. If they exist, we're lucky they seem to want to avoid humans. Those who say they've encountered Bigfoot say the creatures have an eerie presence, make a whistling noise and exude a pungent stench like something rotting.

A second Pacific Northwest ape-like cryptid, although less well known than Bigfoot, is the Agropelter. It is said to be a fearsome mythical creature that is a highly agile climber and inhabits hollow trees of the conifer woods in Oregon. Legend has it the speedy creature awaits unwary people walking by and hurls wooden splinters and branches at them, like Bigfoot throws boulders, while otherwise escaping detection due to its speed. The Agropelter was described by a man named Big Ole Kittleson—who claimed to have survived an Agropelter attack and witnessed the creature escape—as having a skinny, wiry body like an emaciated bear, the face of a gorilla or other type of ape and arms like muscular whips. It uses its hands and arms to break dead branches off trees and throw them through the air like projectiles from a gun. The Agropelter is believed to subsist on woodpeckers, owls and rotten wood. Missing people in the Pacific Northwest's forests are sometimes said to have fallen prey to the Agropelter. When loggers die from tree branches falling on them, Agropelters are blamed. No doubt believing in the Agropelter was a way for pioneers, settlers and others to make sense of strange occurrences taking place in the woods. They are said to be completely black in color, except for the face, which has an ash-gray skull pattern.

BEAR-LIKE CREATURES: GUMBEROO AND BAX

No doubt bears have terrified people throughout history in many parts of the world. Much of this fear is due to the fear of the unknown. Other reasons include exaggerating and demonizing bears to prove one's courage and sell magazines and other media. During the Pleistocene or Ice Age, which ended some twelve thousand years ago, there were huge bears in Asia and elsewhere, much larger than today's. *Arctodus simus*, also known as the giant short-faced and "bulldog" bear because of its short, squat face, which lived from modern-day Alaska to California, was up to twelve feet tall when standing on its hind legs and weighed as much as two tons or 4,000 pounds. The extinction of the mammoths, mastodons and other large herbivores resulted in this huge bear's demise. Some scientists believe these creatures survived beyond the Pleistocene Age, and they no doubt scared humans, who existed at the time and with whom they came in contact, to death. As recently as the early 1920s, a colossal bear skull and huge bear paw prints were found in Sweden. While it's thought these creatures have disappeared, there are legends of outsized bears continuing to exist in remote areas of Siberia. Today, the largest known bears are polar and Kodiak bears, some weighing more than 1,500 pounds and standing almost ten feet tall on their hind legs.

Bears have been portrayed in movies and other media as ranging from the lovable, child-friendly *Winnie-the-Pooh*, based on A.A. Milne's 1926 character, to bloodthirsty beasts. The 2015 Leonardo DiCaprio movie *The Revenant*, featuring a brutal grizzly attack, is based on the real-life history of frontiersman and fur trapper Hugh Glass, who survived a grizzly mauling in 1823. Glass was severely mauled on a journey up the Missouri River and left for dead,

Bear painting, 2023. *Courtesy of Cindy Havenstrite.*

but he survived. A more recent bear movie is 2023's comedy-thriller *Cocaine Bear*, in which a drug-addled killer bear terrorizes the people with whom it comes in contact. The fear of bears has been termed arkoudaphobia. This unfortunately has led to some bear species being driven to near extinction. Since 1960, only about 70 people have been killed by bears in the United States and Canada, with many of these instances taking place in remote areas of Canada. This is compared with about 150 Americans dying each year from hitting a deer while driving.

Given this fear, it isn't surprising that many countries and American states have bear-like cryptids reported. In Africa, there are stories of the Nandi bear, a gigantic, fierce bear-like animal with six toes on each foot and a red fur coat that makes unearthly howls and has been reported to attack and rip humans' heads off. In Asia, the Chinese White Bear is reported to be a pure white bear that lives in the forests, even though bears have been extinct in China for quite some time. In the United States, there is the Alaskan Giant Polar Bear, which is said to be enormous—larger than the Kodiak and the polar bear—with creamy white fur. Also in America, the nineteenth-century frontiersman Grizzly Adams, loosely based on explorer John Capen Adams, and the subject of a 1970s television series, reported a hedgehog-bear covered with spines like a hedgehog. The Elkhorn Monster Bear, with a face resembling a dog, has been reported in Wisconsin. The colorfully named Sheepsquatch, a large, white bear-like creature with goat horns, raccoon-like hands and an opossum's tail that smells of sulfur is said to live in Virginia. The Texas Bear Beast is said to be large, close to four hundred pounds, with red eyes and long foreclaws. It is comfortable on land and in the water and blamed for a dozen human disappearances.

One terrifying account of a deadly bear-like cryptid comes from the 2018 and 2019 American television mini-series *The Terror*, based on a 2007 novel. It is a fictionalized account of the real, doomed and lost 1845–48 arctic exploration of Captain Sir John Franklin and his British Royal Navy ship HMS *Terror* in search of the fabled Northwest Passage across North America. The primary antagonist is the Tuunbaq, a giant, muscular, murderous, shape-shifting Native spirit polar bear–like creature with human facial features that wreaks chaos and death on the ship's crew. The cryptid tears its victims apart and consumes their souls. The creature may be intended to represent the imaginary and real dangers to humans represented by the wild. It may also represent Natives' resentment and desired retribution against White explorers, colonists and settlers who destroyed their villages and world. The mythological creature on which the Tuunbaq is based is the Greenlandic Inuit Tupilaq.

In Pacific Northwest Native cultures, the bear is seen as a symbol of leadership, power, courage and strength. It is no wonder that warriors wore bear claw necklaces as a form of talisman or good-luck charm and protection. There are many legends about bears, including a chief's daughter who was seduced by a bear that could transform into a handsome man. They had two cubs that could also shape-shift into human form. There are also Kitasoo and T'simshian Native stories of the Pacific Northwest's Moksgm'ol or Kermode, which are black bears that are white in color—it is thought there are one to five hundred in existence. They are known as "spirit bears," imbued with magical powers and said to be the keepers of dreams and memories.

In the Pacific Northwest, the black bear is common. I have encountered several since living here, including some huge bears weighing more than six hundred pounds, said to number in Washington and Oregon separately between twenty-five and thirty thousand. These beautiful animals are reclusive and shy. It is estimated only one black bear in a million becomes a predator toward humans, usually as a defensive reaction.

There are also grizzly bears, the other bear found in the lower forty-eight states, in northeastern Washington's Selkirk and North Cascades Mountains; they are rare, numbering only fifty to sixty. There are no grizzly bears in Oregon. Grizzly bears, compared to black bears, are twenty-six times more likely to kill a human.

One of the Pacific Northwest's bear-like cryptids is called the Gumberoo. It has been described as fearsome but rare. The story of the Gumberoo comes from nineteenth-century Pacific Northwest lumberjack tales about a giant bear-like creature. It is said to resemble a fat, potbellied, hairless black bear with prominent eyebrows and bristly chin hair. The creature has leathery, shiny black skin. It's reported to have rows of razor-sharp teeth

Bears, 1913.
Courtesy of Library of Congress.

and is constantly hungry when not hibernating—which it does often—attacking anything that looks like food. Some have been reported eating an entire horse in one sitting. The Gumberoo is said to live in hollowed-out trunks of burned-down cedar trees along the Pacific Northwest coast. In fact, Gumberoo is associated with forest fires and is said to itself be combustible when faced with heat. Woodsmen have reported hearing loud explosions and smelling a burning rubber-like scent in the air with the death of a reported Gumberoo. It's been reported that when a person inhales the smoke left from the explosion of the Gumberoo, their organs become coated with a rubber-like substance. Those who have encountered the Gumberoo report it's immune to bullets, arrows and any other weapon, which are said to bounce off. Its only weakness is fire—the only way to kill it. It is also said to be slow in its movements, allowing for those encountering it to escape.

Another Pacific Northwest bear-like cryptid is the Baxbakwalanuxsiwae—I'll call it Bax for short. This strange creature is a combination of human, bear and other creatures. The Native story is it was once a man, but cannibalism resulted in his being cursed. It now appears as a hairless bear-like human, covered in bleeding mouths screaming "hap, hap, hap"—said to mean "eat, eat, eat." The Bax is also called the Cannibal-at-the-North-of-the-World and lives in a remote cabin. The creature has several helpers who prepare humans to serve as food. Qominaga appears to be Bax's human wife, and Kinqalalala appears to be his human servant. They ensure victims are well fed and comfortable before they become dinner.

The belief in Gumberoo and Bax may be based on many factors, including humans' fear of bears and the danger and unexplainable nature of forest fire—a significant problem in the Pacific Northwest—the fact some bears have been shot several times but do not seem to die, at least not immediately, and a warning against cannibalism.

BIRD-LIKE CREATURES: THUNDERBIRDS AND THE "CROOKED BEAK OF HEAVEN"

Many cultures have folklore and legends about birds and bird-like creatures. Russia has several bird-related legends, including the Alkonost and Sirin, with a woman's head and a bird's body, whose song brought peace. Roman mythology's Caladrius is a snow-white bird that absorbs disease; Asian folklore features the Roc, a giant bird of prey; and the ancient phoenix serves as a

Thunderbird. *Courtesy of Pixabay, ArtSpark.*

symbol of renewal, rising from the ashes. The Pacific Northwest has many legendary, and in one case mythical, birds residing in the region, several with seemingly magical powers. The fear of birds is termed ornithophobia. This fear may have been most dramatically captured in the 1963 Alfred Hitchcock movie *The Birds*, in which birds in a coastal area along the Pacific Ocean inexplicably begin attacking and killing people. A fear of birds took on new meaning when it was realized, first in 1868 by Thomas Henry Huxley but not widely understood until the 1970s, when paleontologist John Ostrom promoted the idea that birds were descended from dinosaurs. In fact, birds are descended from theropods, dinosaurs with hollow bones, with three toes and claws on each limb. This fact was highlighted in the popular 1993 Steven Spielberg movie *Jurassic Park* and made clearer in later installments.

Birds are an important part of Native culture, as they are connected to the earth and heaven or flying realms. In Native American and other cultures, supernatural explanations are often given for events that are not easily explained. Stories of blackbirds, blue jays and Thunderbirds help explain natural phenomena like death, earthquakes and volcanic eruptions.

Blackbirds, common in the Pacific Northwest, are sometimes associated with death, omens of bad things to come and evil. This may be because of their jet-black color, the croaking sound they make or other reasons. As I described in my 2022 book *Monsters and Miracles: Horror, Heroes and the Holocaust*, when my father—a prisoner of the Nazis in World War II—was sick, he dreamed of fighting a large blackbird and won. The next day, other prisoners from his barracks were marched into the woods and killed, while my still sick father stayed behind and survived. An elderly religious man later interpreted my father's dream as his fighting and overcoming death and evil. Some cultures also see black birds as representing tricksters, demigods and the gods and goddesses of myth. Native shamans—tribal healers and holy people who serve as mediums between the physical and spirit world—consider them to be spirit messengers. In the Bible, the blackbird symbolizes temptation, sin, darkness and evil. The Bible says the devil sent the blackbird to tempt humans with worldly desires. Many cultures and religions believed that a blackbird was an omen sent by the gods or higher powers to foretell death. For others, the blackbird was seen as an evil or malignant force. Some believe that seeing a blackbird can signal a change in luck or fortune, positive or negative, a transformation. Seeing one was thought to be lucky, while seeing three together was the opposite. In ancient times, it was believed these birds acted as magical messengers whose warnings were to be heeded to ensure better times. Blackbirds were seen as unlocking life and nature's mysteries through mysterious powers.

To some Pacific Northwest Natives, the blue heron represents self-determination and self-reliance. It is thought of as a lucky charm, as it is a successful fisher. It is also a symbol of grace, patience and elegance. Sighting a heron is also said to prompt humans to look deeper into themselves and access their innate wisdom. Similarly, the loon is thought to symbolize serenity and tranquility, teaching humans to listen to and learn from their dreams.

Chinook Natives of the Pacific Northwest tell the story of the trickster god Blue Jay, who sought and married a woman who had been dead for five days. He found medicine people in the land of the dead who revived the woman, and he became so popular he was elected chief. He eventually brought his wife back to the land of the living, but her father, seeing her alive, demanded Blue Jay cut off and give him his wife's hair as a dowry. Blue Jay refused, turned into a bird and fled back to the land of the dead with his wife.

The Crooked Beak of Heaven is seen by Kwakwaka'wakw Natives as a giant, supernatural bird servant to the aforementioned Baxbakwalanuxsiwae.

It figures prominently as part of the Hamatsa or cannibal dance ceremony, in which Native dancers wear masks that feature a large beak with dramatic curving pieces spiraling off of it.

The bald eagle—I have seen them regularly on the Oregon and Washington coasts and elsewhere in the Pacific Northwest—has served as a national symbol throughout history, for Babylon, Egypt, Rome and today the United States. In Native culture, the eagle conveys the powers and messages of the spirit; the bird flies higher than other birds and forms a connection between man and heaven. It brings the message of renewed life, as it is associated with the east winds—the direction of spring—dawn and rebirth.

The eagle has been an important emblem of national pride for thousands of years. In Greek mythology, the god Zeus changed into the sacred eagle to control lightning and thunder. The ancient Hittites relied on the double-headed eagle so they would never be surprised by unforeseen events. The Aztecs' chief god told the people to settle at a location where they would find an eagle consuming a snake while standing on a cactus. Natives, especially the Pueblo, associated the eagle with the energies of the sun and saw the birds as symbols of greater sight and perception. Natives believe the eagle signals new beginnings and provides stamina and endurance. Further, it is the symbol of honesty and truth. Siberian tribes believe the eagle was the first shaman or medicine person, sent to humankind by the gods to heal sickness and suffering. Some Natives similarly see the hawk as a symbol of courage and strength and honor it.

The bald eagle first appeared as the symbol of America in 1776, when it appeared on a Massachusetts copper cent. It has been the United States' national bird since 1782, when its image was placed on the country's Great Seal. President John F. Kennedy wrote to the Audubon Society about the bald eagle being the United States' representative, saying that the Founding Fathers had made the right decision. He commented on the bird's beauty and independence, emblematic of America's strength and freedom. The bald eagle is protected under the National Emblem Act of 1940. Interestingly, Benjamin Franklin much preferred the turkey as the symbol of America. He observed that the bald eagle had "bad moral character," presumably due to its scavenging and robbing other animals of

Opposite: American eagle, 1898. *Courtesy of Library of Congress, Marcus Wickliffe Baldwin.*

Right: Thunderbird statue, 2018. *Courtesy of Library of Congress, Carol M. Highsmith, photographer.*

their kills. Franklin thought the turkey to be a more respectable bird native to America.

Some Pacific Northwest Natives dance the dance of the grouse for protection, bravery and courage. This bird is known to flap its wings to draw attention to itself and away from its young if danger is nearby and sometimes sacrifice itself to protect its chicks. The grouse represents joy, power, healing and protection. It is thought to be careful, and it warns others to trust their inner spirits.

The hummingbird is seen by some Natives as representing friendship and playfulness and is a symbol of good luck. They are messengers of peace and help humans maneuver life's challenges.

Owls are associated by some Natives with the spirits of deceased ancestors and are treated with respect. They symbolize wisdom and sacred knowledge. Other Natives consider the owl a "boogeyman," again associated with death, but use the animals to scare children into behaving themselves—otherwise they might be carried away into the forest.

The raven is thought by some Natives to be a transformer and trickster—I discuss tricksters in the "Other Native Tales" section. The Kwakwaka'wakw think of the raven as a mischievous glutton. It is adventurous and out to please itself.

Thunderbirds are important in Native culture and are thought of as magical creatures. Virtually every Native American culture, including in the Pacific Northwest, has legends of these giant, powerful, supernatural and magical birds. Native stories of Thunderbirds date back thousands of years. Many of these legends are found in the art, songs and oral histories of various Native cultures. Thunderbirds were said to be close relatives of the ancient Egyptian and Greek phoenix. The former's name is based on the creature's wings making a thunderclap-like sound when in flight. Each wing has been described as larger than a canoe and each feather the size of a paddle. The Thunderbird's eyes glow red in color, and lightning shoots out of its talons. The Thunderbird creates storms when it flies, and at least two Thunderbirds were said to fly in the Pacific Northwest: the first in the Cascade Mountain range and the second in the Olympic Mountains of Washington's Puget Sound. The Thunderbird was said to cause earthquakes and volcanic eruptions on Washington's Mount St. Helens. Some experts believe Natives may have mistaken large eagles, common in the Pacific Northwest, as the legendary Thunderbird. One of the first non-Native accounts dates to 1860, when the Arizona newspaper the *Tombstone Epitaph* published an article about men on horseback who shot a "winged monster" out of the sky. It was described as a pterodactyl-like animal with an eighteen-foot-long wingspan, and a photo purportedly of the creature was included with the story. The Thunderbird is thought to be so impressive; the U.S. Air Force selected the name for its highly skilled precision acrobatic flight demonstration team.

The Lewis and Clark Expedition reported an interaction with a mysterious giant bird. On November 18, 1805, Clark and a party of eleven went to the Washington coast and saw the Pacific Ocean for the first time. One of the men killed a bird with a huge wingspan of over nine feet. Their description corresponds with that of a California condor. It is thought there was a small population of these birds in the Pacific Northwest mountains until they were hunted to near extinction. Some believed the condor may have been mistaken for the Thunderbird. In the late 1960s and early 1970s, several southeast Washington residents reported seeing a large bird with a wingspan like a small private airplane. In 2002, people living in Alaskan villages reported seeing a bird much bigger than anything they had ever seen before. Also in 2002, an airplane pilot carrying passengers to one of these villages said he saw a giant bird with a wingspan of about fourteen feet, the size of a Cessna 207 plane, flying next to his aircraft.

While I was speaking on cryptids and haunted history at a 2022 Halloween event in Astoria, Oregon, at a local brewery, a woman approached me and told of her alarming experience in seeing a huge, pterodactyl-like bird near Mount St. Helens. She was shaken by the experience and swore it was true.

CAT-LIKE CREATURES: BALL-TAILED CAT, KLICKITAT APE CAT AND THE "TWINS"

Many cultures, ranging from ancient Egyptian and Greek to Native, have legends about cat-like creatures. A fear of cats is called ailurophobia. It is thought this fear may be due to a prior traumatic event related to a cat, such as being bitten, or the cat's supposed connection to witchcraft. Believing in cat-like supernatural creatures may be a reflection of the fears humans have had for thousands of years of lions, tigers and other wild, ferocious felines. Some scientists believe early humans coexisted with the large saber-toothed cats or Homotherium, the size of an adult male lion, with giant upper incisor teeth, which went extinct eight to ten

Egyptian cat. *Courtesy of Pixabay, Brew22.*

thousand years ago. Fear of wild Pacific Northwest cats may be related to the unpredictable nature of mountain lions, cougars or pumas, as they're sometimes called, which—while often shy and reclusive—have been known to attack humans. Cougars are the largest cats in the Pacific Northwest, with adult males averaging 140 to 180 pounds, females generally weighing up to 110 pounds, and measuring about seven to eight feet long from nose to tip of tail. Other wild cats in the region include the bobcat and the Canada lynx. I have listed some of the Pacific Northwest cat-like cryptid tales here.

Throughout history, cats have been viewed alternatively as good luck charms and even deities in Egypt and as harbingers of evil related to witch hunts. In both cases, cats have been ascribed supernatural powers. Many of these stories appear to be based on the underlying fear of cats and not real events or interactions. The ancient Romans staged fights to the death between these and other wild creatures, as well as fed Christians to the lions. Some cultures think tiger and other cat body parts have healing and other medicinal properties. It is for these and other reasons, such as trophies from hunts, that large wild cats have been hunted to the brink of extinction. Cats in general have enigmatic personas, making them difficult to understand, mysterious and thought by some not to be trusted. This dislike of cats took a deadly turn in 2018 with a "cat serial killer" in Olympia, Washington, described later.

Cat-like creatures, in movies and other popular media, have been portrayed as Disney cartoon characters such as those in 1970's *The Aristocats*; comic book villains—but also the heroes—Batman's love interest, Cat Woman, in DC Comics, 1940 and beyond; supernaturally charged, dangerous but erotic creatures in 1982's *Cat People*; enigmatic singing characters in the 1982 musical *Cats* by Andrew Lloyd Webber, based on T.S. Eliot's poetry, later a 2019 movie; and others.

The Ball-Tailed Cat is a legend of nineteenth-century Pacific Northwest lumberjacks. The life of a lumberjack was and is difficult and dangerous, facing man-made and natural conditions and unknown threats. Dangers included accidents, the weather, thawing ice, primitive living conditions, other frontiersmen, Natives, bears and mountain lions. A sense of fear was common, and lumberjacks saw risks behind every tree. This cat was said to be a huge, aggressive cat with a heavy stone-like appendage at the end of its tail, almost like an ankylosaur—a heavily armored dinosaur with a hard, bony tail club. It had long claws that it used to help climb trees. It was said to sit and wait for unsuspecting lumberjacks, whom it jumped on and attacked with its tail ball.

Black cats are found in all parts of the world, including the Pacific Northwest. They've been getting a "bad rap" since at least the thirteenth century, when the Catholic Church declared them incarnates of the devil. In most Western cultures, black cats have often unfortunately been seen as symbols of evil omens, suspected of being the "familiars" and minions or servants of witches or shape-shifting witches themselves. It is thought, in many Western cultures, that a black cat crossing your path is an unlucky omen. Interestingly, in Japan the black cat is considered a lucky charm, especially for single women, for whom they are said to bring luck in love. Unfortunately, the fear of black cats has led to many being dropped off at animal shelters. Likewise, owners of black cats—we have had at least one—are particularly protective of their pets on Halloween, when they may be in danger from those thinking they're evil. The fear of black cats may have started in Greece, where black cats were thought to be the companions of witches. In Greek mythology, a goddess of the underworld, Hecate, was a shape-shifter who could turn into a black cat. Over time, Hecate became associated with witches, magic and ghosts. By the medieval era, despite the domestication of cats, the belief black cats were bad luck and

Witch, 2024.
Courtesy of Jason McLean.

associated with witches had spread throughout Europe. In an ironic twist, the mass killing of cats because of superstition had a truly deadly effect on humans, as the rat population which carried the Black Plague or death grew exponentially in the fourteenth century. Unfortunately, when illness or other negative things occurred, the black cat was too often blamed. In Scotland, they were alternately thought of as lucky—seeing one meant you would be coming into money—or fatal: a black cat jumping on a sick person's bed was considered a death omen. In America, dreaming of a black cat was thought to mean the impending death of a family member.

Some Native tribes of the Pacific Northwest say seeing a cougar, mountain lion or puma or hearing its scream is an evil omen. They also see cougars as tied to witchcraft, while other tribes see them as noble animals. It is also associated with powerful hunting medicine.

The Klickitat, named for Klickitat County, Washington, or Ebony Ape Cat has been reported in the Columbia River Gorge of Oregon and Washington. It's described as a large—standing up to five feet at the shoulder, much larger than a mountain lion—and heavily muscled. The cat-like beast has black hair said to stick straight out and a long tail—up to six feet. Some reports say it has been seen standing on its hind legs. It has intelligent ape-like eyes and has been described as a mix of a panther and large monkey. It's also said to

Cougar. *Courtesy of Pixabay, burntpoet.*

be completely unafraid of people. The creature's presence is said to cause electromagnetic disturbances, including causing batteries to die. Those who have seen it say they are instantly aware they are in the presence of something other than a normal animal, a supernatural presence of some kind. Some reports of the Klickitat Ape Cat date back forty years. Klickitat County has embraced the Ape Cat and other reported supernatural activity for tourism purposes. In 2022, I spoke with a man who was leading marketing and tourism efforts related to this cryptid, and he described the large number of residents who claim to have encountered it. Some believe these cat-like creatures are misidentified mountain lions, bobcats or porcupines.

The Pacific Northwest's Splintercat has been reported in Oregon's Cascade Mountain Range. It is said to be a ferocious nocturnal cat-like cryptid that preys on raccoons and bees. It flies between tree branches with great speed and agility, knocking branches off as it hits the next tree. However, this near-constant striking trees with its head, releasing bees and raccoons, has left it with perpetual headaches, putting it in a foul mood—and not to be approached. The creature's name comes from the splintered condition in which it leaves the trees it strikes. Those who have seen this creature say it has very long claws, powerful legs and fur patterned and colored like the bark of its favorite trees. It is a silent creature, until it leaps on its prey. The Splintercat features in Julie Andrews's—yes, the Julie Andrews of *Mary Poppins* and *The Sound of Music* fame—2003 children's book *The Last of the Really Great Whangdoodles*.

The Twins are Pacific Northwest cryptids said to resemble two supernatural black cats. The legend starts with feeding one black cat. The next day, you'll see, seemingly, the same black cat. But they are, in fact, two different cats; one can determine which is which based on personalities. While the first will hiss and refuse to let you approach it, the other will have a calm, serene demeanor. The Twins will appear only in a certain area, like your doorstep or an alley. Many have tried watching where these cats go after they eat, but the Twins need only half a second to disappear until the next mealtime. Taking photographs of them is seemingly impossible, as the photos will just show an empty bowl, no cat in sight.

On a positive note, having cats as pets has been found to lower stress and blood pressure and reduce the risk of heart disease—maybe they are enchanted! There's an old veterinary saying that if you put a pile of broken bones and a cat in the same room, the bones will miraculously heal. Maybe it's because cats seem to meditate, or just sleep a lot, that people and civilizations have attributed mystical qualities to them.

DOG-LIKE CREATURES: WEREWOLVES AND DOGMAN

Dog-like cryptids have been said to inhabit our world since ancient times. In ancient Greece, hellhounds were connected to the legend of Cerberus, the three-headed Underworld guardian—the three-headed dog "Fluffy" in the *Harry Potter* books and movies is modeled after Cerberus. Norse mythology has a similar creature, the Warg, which is a wolf-like creature that destroyed the god Odin in the battle of Ragnarök. These creatures are said to be evil spirits or demons that serve as guardians of forbidden areas and/or how demons enforce contracts with humans—by sending hellhounds to collect their souls.

Dog-like creatures have been the focus of books, television programs, movies and other popular media and are staples of horror stories. These include the werewolf—a human that has transformed into a wolf-man creature—which is one of the longest-existing stories of dog-like cryptids and was featured in 1941's *The Wolfman*, 1981's *An American Werewolf in London* and others. Other dangerous dog-like cryptids have included *Cujo*, Stephen King's 1981 novel and the 1983 horror movie of the same name. However, there have also been upbeat stories involving dogs, including Toto in 1939's *The Wizard of Oz*, the heartwarming story of a collie in *Lassie Come Home*, Disney's 1955 *Lady and the Tramp* and many others.

The Pacific Northwest has several dog-like cryptids. I will spend some time tracing the history of these creatures before getting to those in the Pacific Northwest. I'll start with wolves, on which werewolves are based.

Wolves have been misunderstood and feared in the United States, Europe and elsewhere for as long as can be remembered. They have served as the "bad guys" and untrustworthy "strangers" in literature, including the seventeenth-century "Little Red Riding Hood." No doubt there are historic examples of wolves attacking humans, and certainly livestock, although they'd much rather avoid humans. In North America, there have only been twenty-one documented fatal wolf attacks on humans in recorded history, with fourteen of those in the lower forty-eight states. There are reports elsewhere of larger numbers of humans killed by wolves, including Finland's "Wolves of Turku," a trio of wolves said to have killed twenty-two children in 1880 and 1881, although this is disputed.

The history of wolves in the Pacific Northwest is a sad one, as they were practically hunted to extinction. The last breeding wolves in Washington were eliminated in the 1930s, and the last wolf was killed for a bounty in Oregon in 1947. More recently, with an understanding of the crucial role

Wolf, 1874. *Courtesy of Library of Congress, L. Prang & Co.*

wolves play in the ecosystem, such as keeping the numbers of deer down, wolves have been reintroduced to the Pacific Northwest and elsewhere. As of 2022, according to the Washington Department of Fish and Wildlife and Confederated Tribes of the Colville Indian Reservation, at least 216 wolves in 37 packs lived in Washington State. As of 2022, there were about 178 wolves in Oregon. Pacific Northwest wolves can reach up to six feet in length, including the tail, about thirty inches in height at the shoulder, and males weigh up to one hundred pounds, while females average seventy to eighty pounds.

In a recent act of hatred toward wolves, in February 2024, three endangered gray wolves, two wearing tracking collars, were found killed in Bly in southern Oregon's Klamath County, about three hundred miles southeast of Portland. A $50,000 reward has been offered by a federal agency for information about these illegal killings. It's illegal to hurt or kill gray wolves, as they're protected under the federal Endangered Species Act.

Given the long-standing fear of wolves and a propensity for seeing the unexplainable in supernatural terms, one can imagine how wolves and men were combined to create the monster known as the werewolf. The word *werewolf* comes from Old English and means "man-wolf." The werewolf or lycanthrope—werewolves are termed lycanthropes from the Greek words *lucos*, meaning wolf, and *anthropos*, meaning man—is the best-known dog-like cryptid. The werewolf legend originated in Asia, with the creature's first appearance in 1800 BC (3,823 years ago), in the *Epic of Gilgamesh*, in which the hero spurns a lover because she turned a previous mate into a wolf. Greek mythology also had an early werewolf in the legend of Lycaon—Pelasgus

Werewolf statue.
Courtesy of Pixabay,
Efraimstochter.

angered the god Zeus, and he and his sons were turned into wolves. The Greeks believed the corpses of werewolves, if not destroyed, would return to life as vampires prowling battlefields, drinking the blood of dying soldiers. It is said a person can shape-shift into a wolf-like creature voluntarily, due to a magic spell or curse, or by being bitten by a werewolf. Some legends say this change occurs on the night of a full moon.

The battle of werewolves versus vampires is ages old. The Roma or Gypsies believed werewolves served as protectors of caravans against vampires. Similarly, in Irish lore, there is a story of a priest stricken with lycanthropy who protects travelers from vampires while on the way to a monastery. Cultures differ on how the werewolf condition can be corrected or ended, including ingesting wolfsbane—a poisonous plant said to fight against supernatural creatures—surgery and exorcism. Most legends say a werewolf can be killed by being shot with a silver bullet, with fire, cutting off their heads and removing their heart. Interestingly, some cultures, including Native American, take pride in being descended from wolves. The ancient Romans claimed their empire was established by twin orphaned infants, Romulus and Remus, on April 21, 753 BC, on the site they were suckled by a wolf. The German Nazis of World War II were proud of their supposed ancestry tied to strong and brave wolves, and wanting to scare their enemies, they named their submarine or U-boat fleets wolfpacks and named individual submarines *Wolf*, *Sea Wolf* and *Tearing Wolf*.

A fear of wolves and other dog-like creatures has existed for thousands of years. Throughout history, in Europe, governments literally declared war on wolves. For example, in France in the 800s, the government hired an elite corps of hunters to control the wolf population. In England in the late 1200s, King Edward ordered the extermination of wolves in some parts of the country. In 1427, James of Scotland passed a law requiring three wolf hunts a year. Much of this killing was due to humans' fear of wolves, primarily based on their fearsome reputation. This fear gave rise to cautionary fairy tales, including one of the first wolf-related horror stories: "Little Red Riding Hood." In the story, the "Big Bad Wolf" serves as the antagonist or monster. The wolf is clever, disguising himself as Little Red Riding Hood's grandmother. He's going to eat Red, until the hunter kills him and saves the day.

Those immigrating to the New World in the 1500s and 1600s brought their fear of wolves with them. In America, these fears were exhibited in colonial and pioneer times, mostly based on wolves' terrifying reputation. An estimated 2 million wolves roamed the woods and other areas of North America when colonists first landed. Despite wolves mostly avoiding humans, they were hunted to the brink of extinction. The first bounty in what would become America was offered for hunting wolves in Massachusetts in 1630, with New Jersey following suit in 1697. Historians have estimated the number of wolves killed in America during the 1860s and 1870s at more than 100,000 per year. While wolves were placed on the endangered list in 1974, conservation efforts have been successful in rebuilding their numbers. In the twentieth and twenty-first centuries, wolves were reintroduced to the continental United States, and hunts have again been made legal to control the size of the wolf packs. The current wolf population in the United States is between 14,780 and 17,780, with the majority in Alaska.

According to a 2021 YouGov survey of one thousand American adults, 8 to 9 percent believe werewolves exist. Some researchers believe the fear of werewolves represents the fear of losing control over our own bodies, of looking ugly and beastly in our physical appearance and actions.

In the United States, there are long-standing Native tales based on the dire wolf, a real canine species with a particularly strong bite that was about twenty pounds heavier than the modern-day gray wolf and went extinct about ten thousand years ago. Many people are familiar with the dire wolf through the 1996 novel by George R.R. Martin and the long-running (2011–19) HBO television series based on the book *A Game of Thrones*. In Louisiana, Cajun stories of the Rougarou have scared people for centuries. This creature has been described as having a human body but the head of a dog or wolf. Legend has it the werewolf-like Rougarou was created by the curse of voodoo priestesses. They are said to hunt down Catholics who don't follow the rules of Lent.

One Pacific Northwest dog-like cryptid is the Oregon Woodland Dogman, said to be a menacing hybrid between a Sasquatch and a werewolf. Dogman has been reported living in dark, wooded areas in Oregon. It has been described as seven feet tall with pointy German Shepherd–like ears and a long snout, but human-like facial and torso features. Others have described it as a hellhound with big and sharp teeth, red eyes and an evil grin. This creature has been seen in Albany and Klamath Falls, Oregon.

Many Pacific Northwest Native cultures, including the Quileutes of northwestern Washington, have legends of coyotes, dogs, wolves and dog-like creatures, some relatively benign and others dangerous. The Quileutes believe they are descended from a pair of wolves created by a "transformer" or shape-shifter named Qwati. The tribe celebrates its wolf-related ancestry with wolf dances, dresses in wolf-related costumes and holds other festivities. Author Stephenie Meyer's *Twilight* series, later made into movies, plays off the Quileute legends—many say inaccurately. To many Native peoples, the wolf represents loyalty, intelligence, strong family ties, sociability, understanding and good communication. It is thought of as the land animal with the greatest supernatural powers. Other Natives tell a story of the mischievous spirit named Coyote who infuriated an evil spirit and fled to a mountain to wait out the flood the evil spirit caused. Another Native story about Coyote had the spirit share knowledge and power over fire with the Klamath tribe. Still another Coyote story describes how it helped create the Columbia River Gorge

Native wolf dancers, 1914. *Courtesy of Library of Congress, Lomen Bros., photographer.*

in Oregon and Washington by fighting a giant beaver god whose tail scraped out the Gorge.

It is thought that some of these stories were used to inspire fear and obedience. Other possible reasons for these legends are two real-life medical conditions. The first is called clinical lycanthropy, in which the patient has the delusional belief they are turning into a wolf. The second is called congenital terminal hypertrichosis, which is characterized by fully pigmented terminal hair covering the entire body. It is also called "werewolf syndrome" due to the thick, dark hair that appears.

Finally, although dogs have been considered "man's best friend," based on their loyalty and service for tens of thousands of years, some people just fear dogs. This may be due to real-life experiences or some less well-founded reason. There are some 62 million pet dogs in the United States, so avoiding them may be difficult. As with cat-like creatures discussed earlier, these legends appear to be more closely related to an underlying fear of dogs rather than real events or interactions. A fear of dogs is called cynophobia. Treatment for fear of dogs and other phobias can be undertaken through

Native wolf dancers, 2024. *Courtesy of Jason McLean.*

systematic desensitization, relaxation with imagined situations and in vivo or exposure therapy—systematic and prolonged exposure to a dog without an adverse reaction.

OTHER NATIVE LEGENDS:
DEMONS, WENDIGO AND SKINWALKERS

Natives have lived in the Pacific Northwest for at least ten thousand years. In what is now Washington, the Native tribes have included the Duwamish, Nisqually, Salish, Skagit, Snoqualmie and others. In present-day Oregon, tribes include the Chinook, Clatsop and Tillamook. Many area towns and other landmarks are named for Native tribes. Natives have suffered discrimination, massacres, forced moves, wars, starvation, mass death due to diseases carried by immigrants and other calamities. Natives maintain their legends and stories, passing them down from generation to generation and addressing life, harmony with nature, peace and death. Many of these stories discuss heroes and supernatural beings, as well as animals. Tribes have many different tales of supernatural creatures and beings. The religion of many Pacific Northwest Natives is animistic; they believe in the existence of spirits and souls in all living and some nonliving objects. In other sections, we discuss Pacific Northwest Native tales about the ape-like Bigfoot or Sasquatch, dog-like cryptids, sea serpents, Thunderbirds, the Kohonta (cannibals) and others.

Tales relating to shape-shifting, thought to be the ability to physically transform through a superhuman ability, divine intervention, demonic manipulation, sorcery, spells or some other means are shared by many cultures. We've discussed some well-known shape-shifters, including werewolves. Therianthropy is the term for human-animal shape-shifting. Native shape-shifting may be positive, as practiced by medicine people, or evil, as practiced by so-called Skinwalkers. The idea of the trickster—a god, goddess or other being who demonstrates great intellect and secret knowledge but uses it to play tricks and otherwise disobey rules and conventional

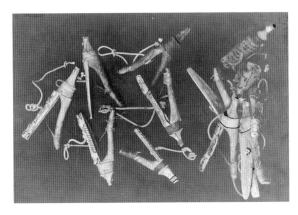

Native fishhooks, 1900.
Courtesy of Library of Congress.

Native totem pole. *Courtesy of Pixabay, ArtTower.*

behavior—is a theme common among several cultures, including Native American. Many Native tales focus on the trickster, which playfully disrupts life, steals possessions and is a mischievous being.

Natives of the Pacific Northwest have several demon-like creatures. Demons are said to be evil, malevolent supernatural entities that make deals with people, giving them what they desire in exchange for their souls. Belief in demons is thought to date back thousands of years, stemming from humanity's fear of the unknown, the strange and the horrific. One way to differentiate a demon from a human is said to be by their eyes, which may flash black, red or some other color. Although there is no universally agreed-on method of fighting against the devil or demons, prayer and exorcism—the attempted expulsion of an evil spirit from a person or place—are sometimes tried. Christianity calls for holy water, water blessed by a religious figure, and religious symbols, including the cross, but one must believe in the power of the symbol, thought to be effective deterrents to possession and weapons against evil entities. Interestingly, according to a 2007 Baylor University Survey, 54 percent of Americans "absolutely" believe demons exist. According to a 2021 YouGov survey of one thousand American adults, 43 percent say they believe demons exist. The Native Mynoghra is described as a "Great Old One, the She-Demon of the Shadows." This cryptid has been described as a huge woman with branch-like horns sprouting from her head and tentacles instead of hair. Witch cults throughout the Pacific Northwest worship her. Her followers are said to have the power to place hexes and cast curses. Legend has it that when one of Mynoghra's followers dies, their spirit takes its place as one of her "shadow wolves." The shadow wolves' howls are said to mark Mynoghra's path and should be avoided.

Somewhat like the Mynoghra is the Tahtahkleah, or "Owl-Woman Monster." Legend has it these creatures were five sisters who were supernaturally large—possibly a theme—women, lived in caves and preyed on humans. Natives said they were the most dangerous beings on earth. It was said that the eye of one of these dead monsters was used to create all owls.

A similar legend is that of the Basket Ogress, also known as the Wild or Giant Woman, who was said to be a giant cannibal monster who caught human children and carried them off in her enormous basket.

The Pacific Northwest Salish tell of Stick Indians, malevolent and dangerous beings living in the forest. They are said to resemble other Natives but are unusually tall, seldom seen, nocturnal and communicate in an almost bird-like manner. They are said to play pranks on villages, including stealing food and men's clothing. The Stick Indians are said to have powers of mental persuasion and can induce dread, confusion and anxiety, sometimes through whistling. Some tribes say Bigfoot is a form of Stick Indian. Some tales say these beings kidnap Natives, especially children, to serve as their slaves.

Native tribes have other wide-ranging beliefs and tales, many of which attempt to explain natural and other phenomena that are not otherwise easily explained. The Great Spirit is the basis of Native belief and is made up of multiple deities. Natives appeal to these spirits at every step of their lives and hear them on the wind, see them in the clouds, fear them in the strange sounds they hear and find their creations awe-inspiring.

The Kwakiutl and other Native peoples believe in Bukwus or Pukmis, a drowned, skeletal, long-haired ghost-like figure also called the Wild Man of the Woods, Man of the Sea and King of Ghosts. He attracted the ghosts of others who have drowned. He also tried to persuade living humans to consume ghost food to become like him. Some claim Bukwus and Bigfoot are in fact the same creature, although others dispute it.

The story of Kohonta is a Native tale about a human who engaged in extensive cannibalism and was punished by his tribe. A shaman cursed the person to shape-shift into a creature with an insatiable hunger that is bound by magic to be trapped in certain areas of forest. The Kohonta roams through the forest, starving, looking for its next human meal. This creature is like the Wendigo, with the difference being the Kohonta was cursed before it could become a Wendigo.

The Wendigo legend is from Algonquin Native lore of the northeastern and central part of the United States and Canada; its name means "the evil that devours." It started as an ordinary man who, to survive, turned to cannibalism, which turned it into a monster that preys on people as food. The Wendigo is described as large and furry, with big eyes and a skinny body; it walks on two legs and is forever hungry. Lore says the spirit of the Wendigo can possess people and induce them to cannibalism. Further, it was said if a human turned to cannibalism, the act itself invited being possessed by a Wendigo. The Algonquin Natives employed the phrase "Wendigo psychosis" to explain rare cases of cannibalism, resulting from the belief that one is possessed by a Wendigo. The Skookum is a similar cannibalistic legend of the Oregon Chinook Natives, said to be an evil spirit. The Wendigo has been featured in television programs such as *Supernatural* (2005) and others.

There are stories of shape-shifters in Native, European and American history. All too often these creatures are said to have a malevolent purpose. Somewhat like defeating other cryptids, cutting off the creatures' head may work, as may silver bullets and other weapons.

In Greco-Roman history, shape-shifting is included in Ovid's *Metamorphoses*: Circe, a goddess, transforms the Greek king of Ithaca, Odysseus's men into pigs in *The Odyssey*. Apuleius's Lucius becomes a donkey in *The Golden Ass*. The Oceanid Metis, first wife of Zeus and mother of the goddess Athena, was said to be able to change her appearance to whatever she wanted. Also, in Greek mythology, the gods transformed humans who angered them—Zeus transformed King Lycaon of Arcadia and his children into wolves. In British, Chinese, Indian (Asian subcontinent), Irish, Japanese, Norse and many other cultures' folklore, fairies, witches, wizards and other supernatural beings were known to shape-shift.

Native lore says shape-shifting is a way people can become in tune with nature, bonding with animals they identify with. These may be bears, eagles, wolves and others. Further, anyone can shape-shift—with hunters traditionally being people who do so. Tribal elders and medicine people also shape-shifted to protect, heal and aid their people. Shape-shifting often occurs during song, dance, ceremonies and rituals. Tribe members might dress in feathers or animal furs to better become the animal they are portraying. Dressing in sheepskin, leather and buckskin is generally acceptable, but dressing in the pelt of a predatory animal is typically not, as it lends itself to becoming a Skinwalker. Shape-shifting is thought to be tied to freedom, strength and connecting with the ancestors and spirituality. The shape-shifter changes into the animal that most closely aligns with the person's qualities—strength, kindness and so on. A shape-shifter—which the person becomes, at least mentally—is different from a spirit animal, which is a separate entity that helps a person on their journey.

One Pacific Native shape-shifter is named Kushtaka. It was once human but, as a punishment for a misdeed, was transformed into a large land otter or some other marine creature with the head of an otter and body of a beaver. It is said to have glowing eyes and red fur and is sometimes seen wearing clothing and jewelry. Some Natives say it can speak in human languages and sings beautiful songs. Natives see the Kushtaka as a guardian, leading people away from dangerous places and situations. It also is seen as a mediator, helping animals and people resolve conflict and achieve peace. Its ability to transform humans and creatures into other types of beings has caused some fear. This cryptid has been seen in modern times, with one elderly Washington woman reporting being chased by a large, glowing, strangely scented creature late at night through her garden. The Kushtaka has been featured in modern video games, such as *World of Warcraft*.

The Lushootseed, Natives of Puget Sound—and part of the Coastal Salish people, which includes many tribes—believe the world is full of spirits, including seemingly inanimate objects, such as rocks and weather. These spirits provide lessons, skills and knowledge on how to survive and flourish. Other spirits include Clam or Duck, who help with hunting; Wolf and Thunder, who help undertakers and orators; and Otter, Kingfisher and a giant horned serpent who help individuals become doctors. The Lushootseed were thankful for the resources provided by the spirits, including the shorelines, rivers, prairies, forests and mountains. They believe a transformer or changer named Dukwibal used his power to change people, animals and the land, creating and bringing balance to the world and shaping the world's land masses into their current shapes.

A less benevolent or positive shape-shifter in Native lore is the Skinwalker— found in the Pacific Northwest and elsewhere. As I mentioned earlier, in 2022, the word *Skinwalker* was the most searched cryptid term—over 4 million times, more than Bigfoot—in the United States on Google. Navajo

Native oral history calls these beings *yee naaldlooshii*, which translated means "it goes on all fours." They are said to represent the antithesis or opposite of Navajo cultural values and may be the scariest creatures in Native mythology. Skinwalkers—who are viewed as both shape-shifters and witches—are seen as evil and corrupt, performing harmful ceremonies and manipulative magic in a perversion of the good works medicine people traditionally perform. They direct spiritual forces to cause misfortune and harm to others. The Navajo also refer to this as the "Witchery Way," using corpses for tools and spells used to curse, harm or kill their victims. The word *witch*, from the Western Civilization perspective, comes from Old English and is over one thousand years old. It's a combination of wiccecraeft from *wicce* "witch" and *craeft* "craft." In the medieval and early modern eras, 1400s–1700s, Christianity and other major religions taught their adherents the devil could empower witches, in exchange for their loyalty, and the witches could then harm their neighbors. Those suspected of witchcraft were intimidated, banished, attacked, prosecuted and put to death. Between 1400 and 1782 alone, approximately forty to sixty thousand individuals—mostly women—were killed in Europe and America on suspicion of being witches. One was considered a witch if she used magic to harm another, if it was used by the witch against her own community, if the act was immoral and included working with the devil or some other evil being. A witch either inherited her power or was initiated to it, and the witch's spell could be overcome through a counterspell or punishment of the presumed witch. Some theories say witches can't set foot on hallowed ground, like that around and in a church and a cemetery.

The Navajo and other Pueblo people, including the Apache, Hopi, Ute and others, have their own version of Skinwalkers. Sometimes these malevolent beings evolved or devolved from respected medicine people and spiritual guides. They can be either male or female but are more often men. They became Skinwalkers through a secret initiation, requiring an evil deed, including killing a close family member. An evil group is thought to gather in dark caves and secluded places to conduct this initiation. Other occurrences at these dark gatherings include necrophilia with female corpses, cannibalism, incest and robbing graves. The Skinwalker leader is typically an older man who has lived a long time as a Skinwalker. The Skinwalker can turn into, possess or disguise themselves as animals, most often as coyotes, wolves, foxes, cougars, dogs and bears. Their supernatural powers include extreme speed and agility. The Skinwalker kills others due to greed, anger, envy, spite and revenge. They must continually kill others or die themselves. It is thought

Navajos, 1904. *Courtesy of Library of Congress, Gerhard Sisters, photographer.*

Skinwalkers can possess humans if that person locks eyes with them, causing them to say and do things they wouldn't otherwise say or do. Skinwalkers' other powers include the ability to read minds, control others' thoughts and behaviors, cause illness and disease, destroy property and kill. One way to differentiate a Skinwalker from humans is by their eyes, which are believed to turn bright red—much like some demons—when light is shone on them. Those who say they've encountered Skinwalkers describe strange knocks on windows, banging on walls and scraping noises on the roof, like ghosts.

During times of great adversity, including wars with the U.S. Army, a greater number of tribe members have turned to shape-shifting to try to escape their disastrous existence. At various times in Native history, including the Navajo Witch Purge of 1878, in which forty suspected Skinwalkers were killed by fellow tribe members to restore balance, tribal members have blamed Skinwalkers for their terrible conditions. The Navajo believe these Skinwalkers exist alongside humans. Some of the earliest Skinwalkers can be found in Mayan history: the Mestaclocan was thought to have the ability to change its appearance and manipulate the minds of animals.

The supposed Skinwalker Ranch, located in northeast Utah and near a Native Ute reservation, became an area of focus on Skinwalkers in the 1990s. This ranch has a history of reported UFOs, alien encounters, cattle mutilations and crop circles. The Utes say the Navajo put a curse on their tribe that has plagued the Ute people with Skinwalkers. These events and creatures are featured in the History Channel's television series *The Secret of Skinwalker Ranch*, 2020 to present.

Native law says when a person becomes a Skinwalker, they forfeit their humanity and right to live and should be killed. But Skinwalkers are said to be very difficult to kill, and trying to do so may result in the Skinwalker retaliating. Killing a Skinwalker requires the help of a powerful shaman or medicine person who can invoke spells and rituals, turning the Skinwalker back on itself. Another way to kill a Skinwalker is to shoot the creature in the neck or head with bullets dipped in white ash. Navajo generally won't speak with those outside the tribe about Skinwalkers out of fear of angering the creatures.

Tricksters exist in the myths of many different cultures. The trickster is said to cross and break both physical and societal rules, violating social principles and natural order, playfully disrupting life, stealing possessions, causing mischief and reestablishing life on a new basis. This often takes the form of tricks or thievery, with the trickster being cunning and/or foolish. The trickster openly questions, disrupts and mocks authority.

In Native lore, tricksters were considered clowns and essential to sacred practices, as people couldn't pray until they had laughed. This is because laughter was thought to open and free the individual from rigid preconceptions. The tribe had to have tricksters exist within the most sacred rituals for fear tribe members would forget the sacred comes through upset, reversal and surprise. Natives held the trickster essential to creation and to birth. In Native traditions, tricksters were villains in one story, only to appear as heroes in the next. Two spirits in Native lore that are seen as tricksters, jokesters and pranksters were the Coyote and Raven, who stole fire from the gods. We discussed the Raven, thought to be a trickster, in the bird-like creature section. In Native creation stories, Coyote teaches humans how to catch salmon.

Interestingly, while some Native cultures find value in the existence of clown-like tricksters, clowns have become something to be feared in American and some other cultures. Some—I don't share this view— believe that under the happy, playful makeup of a clown, some individuals are in fact demonic entities intent on hurting and killing the unsuspecting,

Clowns, 2024. *Courtesy of Jason McLean.*

especially children. In 2016, ahead of Halloween, a clown hysteria took place in the United States, including in the Pacific Northwest, and around the world after a series of scary clown sightings became a social media frenzy. Some people, it seems, decided to dress up as clowns to scare others. Some of these "clowns" carried knives, sticks and other weapons. Fear of clowns is called coulrophobia, and it is more common than a fear of heights. It's not clear if it's oversized painted-on lips, accentuated or painted-on eyebrows, the distorted face, a bizarre costume or unpredictable and at times mischievous behavior cause the fear. The 1970s American serial killer John Wayne Gacy performed as Pogo the clown at charitable events and children's parties. He said, "Clowns can get away with murder." Gacy was later found guilty of thirty-three murders in the Chicago area and executed at age fifty-two.

Many of these tales, including those about shape-shifters and tricksters, have been told to explain that which is otherwise difficult to explain. This includes explaining the evil and bad behavior of tribal members, crises that have befallen tribes and other devastating circumstances that have devastated Native communities. It is in some ways easier to blame supernatural shape-shifters and tricksters for these circumstances rather than some other natural reason, including human behavior.

The 2022 movie *Prey*, the fifth installment in the *Predator* franchise—the first in the series was 1987's *Predator* with Arnold Schwarzenegger—took the unique approach of having the extraterrestrial monster fight against Natives of the North American Great Plains of 1719. The movie, with a Comanche producer and Sioux lead actor, is credited with breaking new ground for its authentic portrayal of eighteenth-century Natives. It also takes the folkloric themes of Native lore and cryptids to a whole new level.

Sea Serpents and Marine Creatures: Colossal Claude, Caddy the Cadborosaurus and the Devil's Lake Monster

Legends of sea monsters exist in many parts of America. Greek, Norse, biblical and other folklore talk about sea monsters. Some of the best-known creatures are the kraken, the mythical sea monster able to sink ships and with a taste for human flesh, and the leviathan, an even bigger and more powerful biblical sea serpent able to swallow entire oceans. Natives' oral histories describe fantastic sea creatures that are snake, dragon and dinosaur-like. Those who believe these stories say they may be plesiosauruses—extinct marine reptiles from the Mesozoic and Jurassic ages—that somehow survived. Scientists say those ancient creatures were 5 to 49 feet long and were some of the largest apex predators, with a skull length of 7.3 to 9.4 feet.

Sea and other water-based creatures have been featured in horror and even romantic movies, including 1954's *The Creature from the Black Lagoon* and 2017's *The Shape of Water*. One of the most famous movie and marine monsters was the huge, vengeful shark in Peter Benchley's 1974 book and the 1975 Steven Spielberg movie of the same name: *Jaws*. I can honestly say that, like many other people, I have never felt comfortable swimming in the ocean since seeing *Jaws*.

The Pacific Northwest has more than its fair share of reported sea serpents and other marine cryptids. Some of these stories proved true, as mentioned, giant and colossal squid have been discovered in Puget Sound and the Pacific Ocean, reaching a length of up to forty-six feet and weighing in excess of 1,100 pounds.

Some of the earliest sightings of sea monsters in North America occurred off Cape Ann and Nahant, Massachusetts, in 1638, which makes sense, as they, along with Virginia, were some of the first areas visited and settled by White settlers. The creature was described as one hundred feet in length, with a shaggy head and goggling eyes. In the late eighteenth century, revenue cutters—precursors to the U.S. Coast Guard—were ordered to watch for the sea monster. One fisherman said he emptied his duck gun into the serpent's head, but the creature swam away. Similar creatures have been witnessed in New York's Silver Lake near Gainesville in 1855, in Pennsylvania's Wolf Pond in 1887, in 1890 in one of the Twin Lakes in Massachusetts's Berkshire Hills—where I grew up—and in Devil's Lake in Wisconsin in 1892.

Some people who believe sea serpents exist speculate that a group of plesiosauruses—extinct large marine reptiles from the Mesozoic and Jurassic ages—survived and live in the Columbia River and other Pacific Northwest waterways. Scientists believe the plesiosaurus went extinct in the Cretaceous-Paleogene event that killed off the dinosaurs about 66 million years ago. Those who believe the theory say at least one of these creatures survived in

Sea serpent, 2024. *Courtesy of Jason McLean.*

Men on a beach with a sea serpent sculpture, 1906. *Courtesy of Library of Congress, W.M. Horton.*

the deeper parts of the Columbia River, feeding on the salmon that populate its waters.

The oral histories of Pacific Northwest Natives, including the Kwakwaka, Tlingit and Haidas tribes, describe fantastic sea creatures with names such as Sisiutl and Wasgo. There are ancient petroglyphs in the Pacific Northwest drawn of sea serpent–like creatures. The legends are based along the coasts of Vancouver Island—across from Washington, British Columbia and southeast Alaska—and these creatures are described as large and snake-like. The first non-Native sightings of sea serpents were reported in newspapers and publications, including the *Sunday Oregonian*'s 1905 "Caught by a Savage Sea Toad," the *Oregon Sunday Journal*'s 1906 "Sea Serpents Are Not Summer Resort Delusions," the *Oregonian*'s 1911 "The Great White Serpent of the Malorili: A Tale of Love and Adventure" and the *Oregonian*'s 1913 "Sea Serpents: They Are a Reality and Not a Myth."

The Amhuluk comes from the folklore of the Kalapuya Native people of Oregon. It is said to be a horned dragon, covered in spotted fur, that lives in the area's waterways. It has been blamed for drowning people, causing disease and generating a "malarial fog." Descriptions of the creature range from giant eels bound together to a semi-humanoid being with four legs, a body made of a mass of dead plants that resemble logs and tree root-like feet. The Amhuluk is said to have a dark blue fish-like face with large, yellow glowing eyes and eight smaller eyes encircling the larger eyes. Its teeth are long and sharp, and its throat glows with a bluish color. The tongue is narrow and stinger-tipped, with two sets of backward-facing squid-like tentacles protruding from its head. The Amhuluk features in the 2019 movie *Godzilla: King of the Monsters*.

One of the better-known Pacific Northwest sea serpents, primarily seen in and around the Columbia River that separates Oregon and Washington, is nicknamed Colossal Claude. An eyewitness, First Mate L.A. Larson aboard the lightship tender *Rose*, was the first to report the creature in 1934. He, as well as Captain J. Jensen of the *Rose*, described it as forty feet long with an eight-foot-long neck, a "mean-looking" tail and a snake-like head. Captain Jensen also told the *Morning Oregonian* newspaper that the snake-like creature's head looked more like a camel than a snake but agreed on most other details. A few years later, in 1937, the sea serpent was again in the news. The crew of the fishing trawler *Viv* reported they observed Claude and that the serpent had spent time studying them up close. Captain Charles Graham of the *Viv* described it as a tan, hairy, forty-foot-long creature with a horse-like head. A few months after the *Viv* sighting in 1937, the Whites, a couple visiting the "Devil's Churn," a narrow inlet of the Pacific Ocean 120 miles to the south, reported sighting the creature. The Whites saw, just offshore, what they described as a fifty-five-foot-long, hairy, giraffe-like creature whose head and neck were sticking fifteen feet out of the water. The creature headed south along the coast, and the Whites, hoping to catch a second glimpse, ran to their car and raced after it as it made for Heceta Head—a one-thousand-foot-tall headland above the Pacific Ocean. There, they again sighted the sea serpent before it turned and headed out to sea.

On April 13, 1939, the crew of the fishing boat *Argo* reported the closest sighting yet of the creature as it made its way through the Columbia River. Captain Chris Anderson reported the creature passed within ten feet of the *Argo*, its head and neck rising ten feet above the waves. Anderson said one of his crew members used a boat hook to try to poke the creature, but Anderson stopped him out of fear of agitating the creature and it sinking the boat. The captain observed that the creature had a camel-like head, coarse gray fur and glassy eyes. The *Argo*'s was the last "confirmed" sighting of the Columbia Bar Sea Serpent. No additional recorded sightings of Colossal Claude occurred until 1989. That year, a fishing crew was dragging a net when it snagged on something. The snag started to pull the bow of the ship downward into the water. Captain Donald Riswick was finally able to pull the net in and found a hole had been torn in it. The net was several hundred feet long, had been snagged at about thirty feet deep and had a tear in it that was several feet

People on a beach watching a schooner, 1903. *Courtesy of Library of Congress, Detroit Publishing Co.*

across. These incidents were attributed, by those speculating on this theory, to a giant serpent. Riswick's spotting was the end of the reported sightings in the northwest Oregon and southwest Washington portions of the Columbia River. Rumor has it the creature moved on to other parts of the Columbia River or the Pacific Ocean. Others have speculated that Colossal Claude is some sort of large jellyfish, while others continue to argue that it is left over from the prehistoric era. No one knows what type of cryptid Colossal Claude is. As with Bigfoot and the Loch Ness Monster, science has yet to prove or disprove Colossal Claude's existence. The brewery that hosted the 2022 Astoria Halloween event I mentioned speaking at produces an IPA named for Claude and other brews celebrating local cryptids.

Also in the Columbia River, at Astoria, Oregon, Finnish immigrants blamed the October 1883 disappearance of the sixty-six-foot-long schooner and pilot boat *J.C. Cousins* and the loss of its four-member crew, who were never found, to the Finnish cryptid known as the Tursas. This sea monster was said to be a gargantuan, fierce octopus-type creature related to the mythical kraken. Prior to the boat and crew's disappearance, Astorians watching from the coast described how the vessel zig-zagged across the waves in a strange and some said "possessed" manner.

Another Pacific Northwest sea serpent is named Caddy the Cadborosaurus. It has been reported in the Puget Sound region, from Olympia, Washington, in the south to the Strait of Juan de Fuca Strait in the north forming the United States–Canada border between Washington and Vancouver Island. Like other sea serpents, Caddy has been described as a long green or brown serpent-like creature with multiple bumps on its back and a head like a camel or horse. The first accounts of this creature may lie in ancient Native petroglyphs around the Salish Sea—the part of the Pacific Ocean that includes the San Juan Islands and Washington's Puget Sound, up to the Strait of Juan de Fuca. The Manhousat Natives called the creature Hiyitl'lika. The first White settler accounts date to the late 1800s. In 1937, a strange creature's lifeless body was discovered in the stomach of a sperm whale caught near British Columbia, Canada, and photographed. With hundreds of reported sightings in the last two centuries, which continue, Caddy has been seen by experienced sailors and ordinary people alike. Some believe Caddy might be a type of living prehistoric whale known as a basilosaurus, but most explanations classify it as an oarfish or groups of sea lions. Adding fuel to the belief in Caddy, in 1995, volume 1 of the *Amphipacifica: Journal of System Biology* was published, discussing the Cadborosaurus "serpent." The authors labeled the creature, if it exists, in the *reptilia*—reptiles class—but said it could also be a mammal. In the article, the authors discussed the 1937 event and photo just mentioned.

The M'de Wakan, also known as the Devil's Lake Monster, is a Nakota Sioux cryptid from Devil's Lake in Lincoln County, Oregon. It is a huge, hairy, squid-like monster that attacks and sinks ships. In 1950, the beast was allegedly found, although no evidence was maintained. Legend has it the monster sank a canoe with seven people on board, killing them, some one hundred years ago.

Wallowa Lake is a ribbon lake, a narrow body of water one mile south of Joseph, Oregon. There are two separate cryptids said to live in and around the lake. Natives in the area have spoken of the Wallowa Lake Monster—nicknamed "Wally"—for hundreds of years. It was first reported when the son and daughter of two warring tribes' chiefs, the Nez Perce and Blackfoot, were said to be in forbidden love and met in canoes on the lake, only to be killed by the beast. The monster is said to have a long, snakelike body about fifty feet long, with a head resembling a hippo or a large hog. The second set of cryptids are termed "giant saltwater crustaceans" and are said to be gigantic crab-like creatures. These cryptids were first reported by early Oregon settlers and allegedly moved to Oregon Coast remote locations from elsewhere.

"Marvin" the sea serpent was originally spotted in the Columbia River in 1963. That year, Shell Oil Company divers searching for oil observed the fifteen-foot animal and recorded the encounter on tape. Some believe Marvin and Claude are the same creature. During a viewing of the recording, observers gave the creature the nickname "Marvin the Monster." Adding to the description of Claude, they indicated the creature had barnacled bumps and ridges and swam in a spiral motion in over 180 feet of water. Some of

America's leading marine biologists have studied the recording and debated how to explain what was observed.

The Ogopogo is another sea serpent that has reportedly been spotted in the Pacific Northwest. It has been seen swimming in the sixty-mile-long Lake Chelan in north-central Washington, a gorgeous lake surrounded by the jagged Cascade Mountains. It is described as a creature with a long, powerful tail. Reports of sightings date back more than 150 years. Some say either the same or a similar creature has been observed swimming in Lake Okanagan, British Columbia.

The Pacific Northwest Tree Octopus is said to be a 1998 internet hoax. This elusive creature has been reportedly seen scrambling along mossy branches in Washington's Olympic Peninsula's rainforests. They are said to have originated in the waters of Puget Sound. According to urban legend, the tree octopus spends its early life and mating season in an aquatic environment but moves to the trees later in life, where it hunts small invertebrates, frogs, rodents and insects. Activists claim that the species is threatened by Sasquatch predation, as well as decimation of their habitat by logging, suburban encroachment and other natural predators, such as bald eagles. They say immediate action is needed to save it, including participation in "tree octopus awareness marches" and donations to the conservation organization Greenpeas—a further indication of it being a hoax, misusing the conservation group Greenpeace's name. The urban legend and stories persist of these more than foot-long cephalopods being real. They're also said to have the largest brain-to-body ratio of any octopus. Some call these creatures the "devil of the trees" and a danger to loggers—however, there is no evidence of this. It is reported these creatures can change the color of their skin, with red indicating anger, white fear and a mottled brown tone otherwise.

Octopus, 1898. *Courtesy of Library of Congress, George Grantham Bain Collection.*

The Tacoma Narrows Bridge Octopus, a giant Pacific octopus that creeps along the bottom of the Puget Sound, is a living creature. Over the course of its three- to four-year lifespan, the cephalopod can grow to weigh 150 pounds with arms stretching more than twenty feet. But local lore tells of an even larger creature: a 600-pound "King Octopus" that spooks divers in the murky waters beneath the Tacoma Narrows bridge. At that size, this creature would be more like a colossal squid, which, as mentioned earlier, can reach a length of up to forty-six feet and weights exceeding 1,100 pounds; however, there is no proof of the presence of a colossal squid at this location. Some say the wreckage of the original bridge, called Galloping Gertie due to its wildly undulating movement in high wind, which collapsed during a November 1940 windstorm, provides a perfect habitat for the giant, whose massive tentacles have been seen reaching up out of the water—sounds like a monster movie! The mythical King Octopus has become something of a Tacoma mascot, with a local brewery creating an IPA in the creature's honor.

The Willatuk Sea Serpent is said to travel between Lake Washington and Puget Sound via a secret tunnel. It's Washington's own version of the Loch Ness Monster. This cryptid was dreamed up by Seattle filmmaker Oliver Tuthill Jr., who admitted to it not being real. Based on Native sea serpent legends and his own fascination with the Loch Ness Monster, Oliver created a backstory for the creature and even made a film about it. *Willatuk: The Legend of Seattle's Sea Serpent* won a STIFFY, Seattle's True Independent Film Festival Award, in 2010. Although the existence of the Willatuk Sea Serpent, given Tuthill's admission, is dubious, it fits with the great number of sea serpents reported in the Pacific Northwest.

Adding to the Pacific Northwest's long-standing stories of strange sea cryptids are the lancetfish, a dinosaur-like creature with slithery scaleless bodies and fangs, several of which washed ashore on Oregon beaches in 2023. Also, a strange blob, believed to be a decomposing whale or other large sea creature, washed ashore on the Oregon coast near Florence in 2022.

VAMPIRIC CREATURES: VAMPIRES, BATSQUATCH AND CHUPACABRA

In Stephenie Meyers's 2005–8 book series *Twilight*, and in movies based on them, vampires are said to inhabit Forks and other northwestern parts of Washington. Their existence there, in part, was said to be due to the cloudy,

Above: Bat. *Courtesy of Pixabay, Johannalris.*

Opposite: Vampire, 2024. *Courtesy of Jason McLean.*

rainy conditions, perfect for vampires who wish to avoid the sunlight; Meyers picked Forks based on a Google search that showed Forks as the rainiest town in the lower forty-eight states. In the books and movies, the vampires are portrayed fighting against and in some cases alongside their ancient enemies, werewolves. The movies were filmed in Oregon and Washington, and Forks holds an annual vampire and werewolf festival, celebrating the books and movies. I have toured Forks, and the number of vampire- and werewolf-related displays is impressive.

The organization Lawn Love, which previously published a detailed study on the best U.S. cities to survive a zombie apocalypse—and places where you're most likely to spot Bigfoot—enlisted experts on vampires to compile a 2023 list of the best places to find them. Ranking the five hundred largest cities in America, they found the Pacific Northwest has many cities that make great homes for vampires: Portland, Oregon, came in at number 7 and Seattle at number 9. Other Pacific Northwest cities were ranked high in the listing. Lawn Love applied five factors in reaching their conclusions: food and drink (number of potential victims, blood centers, slaughterhouses, etc.), lair safety (casket suppliers, cloud cover, etc.), deterrents (sunshine, number of churches, etc.), entertainment (vampire-friendly clubs, etc.) and community

(vampire groups, etc.). Interestingly and possibly inexplicably, New York City—site of the FX television series *What We Do in the Shadows*—came in at number 1. Other big cities with lots of potential victims—Chicago, Los Angeles and Philadelphia—were in the top five. Arizona ranked the lowest with its plentiful sunshine.

Vampires are some of the best-known staples of horror movies and longest-existing undead creatures and known for feeding on the living by sucking their blood. They have been thought of as mythical creatures in the Middle East, Europe and elsewhere for thousands of years. One of the first vampires was Alukah, meaning "blood-lusting monster," which appeared in Proverbs 30 of the Bible. Some of the creation myths of vampires are that they are created when an evil being dies or someone dies by suicide, by witches or by the possession of a corpse by an evil spirit or that they are created when someone is bitten by an existing vampire. As mentioned earlier in talking about werewolves, the Greeks believed the corpses of werewolves, if not destroyed, would return to life as vampires prowling battlefields, drinking the blood of dying soldiers.

The idea of a charismatic and sophisticated vampire was created in 1819 by English writer John Polidori with his short story "The Vampyre." Bram Stoker's 1897 book *Dracula*—and the 1931 movie of the same name, starring Bela Lugosi—is thought of as the quintessential vampire story and served as the model for subsequent vampire books and movies. Vlad the Impaler— also called Vlad Tepes or Vlad Dracula, a Romanian leader who was born in 1428 and died in 1477—is thought to have served as Stoker's model for Dracula. As his nickname suggests, he impaled his victims by piercing their bodies on top of wooden stakes placed in the ground.

In America, few people realize the practice of cremation—which, in the twenty-first century, has overtaken burial as the funeral rite of choice—was started in the 1870s for both sanitary reasons and to stop vampirism. Retired Civil War colonel Henry Steel Olcott, who is credited for introducing cremation in America, observed there were no vampires reported in places like India, where Hindu practices called for burning the dead, while there were in countries where the dead are buried.

Several mass vampire hysteria events or panics took place across Europe and America in the late 1700s and 1800s. Corpses thought to belong to vampires were unearthed and a stake driven through their hearts. The panics were often tied to outbreaks of disease. For example, outbreaks of tuberculosis were at times blamed on vampires, with residents digging up the recent dead who were suspected of being vampires and spreading the

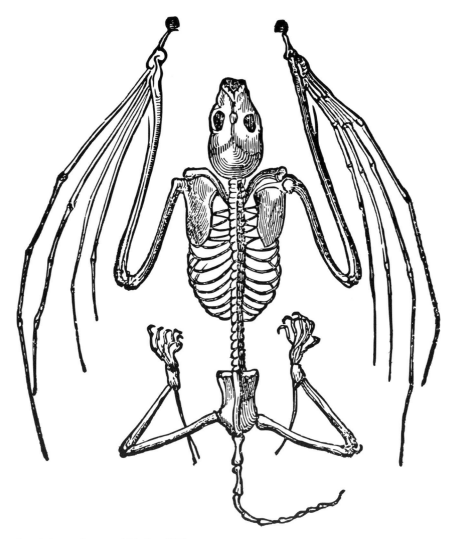

Bat skeleton. *Courtesy of Pixabay, GDJ.*

disease. They beheaded or dismembered the bodies, often burning the dead person's heart. Specifically, in the 1892 Mercy Brown case in Exeter, Rhode Island, members of the Brown family lost their lives to tuberculosis. Residents convinced the Brown patriarch, George, to permit the exhumation of the family's recent dead. Two family members' skeletons were found, but nineteen-year-old Mercy, whose body was preserved by the winter's cold, was found in lifelike form. The residents identified Mercy as a vampire, burned her liver and heart and mixed her ashes in a drink for her brother

Edwin, who died two months later. There were other cases of supposed American vampirism.

Protection from vampires is said to include garlic, crucifixes, holy water, walking on holy ground and driving a stake through the vampire's heart. Ways to prevent the dead from becoming vampires include cutting off the head and burying it between the knees or feet of the corpse, placing a stone in the mouth of the corpse—so they can't bite anyone—burying the corpse upside down, burying a cross with the corpse and burying the corpse with rice or millet, which, it was thought, it would have to count. Some theories about vampires say they avoid and can be "killed" by sunlight. It is said they sleep during the day, to avoid sunlight, in a coffin containing dirt from their home country. It is also said vampires do not cast images in mirrors. A recent (March 2024) news report indicates a Lincoln City, Oregon man stabbed his mother to death with a stake because he believed she was a vampire. He was covered in blood when sheriff's deputies arrived to arrest him. They found his mother's body nearby with a large wooden stake sticking out of her throat. He said his mother would often poke him at night and he would wake with blood on his bedding—he killed her to protect himself. The man has been charged with second-degree murder. Truth is stranger than fiction?

The Pacific Northwest has several vampire-like cryptids. The Batsquatch is described as half-ape and half-bat and said to reside in the forests near Washington's Mount St. Helens. They are described as aggressive, nine-foot-tall creatures with bat-like wings that are up to fifty feet in length. The Batsquatch is said to have hands and feet that resemble bird claws, with hard, leathery skin and talons. Their bodies are covered in blue-colored fur, and their head resembles that of a yellow-eyed wolf, with sharp teeth. Like vampires, they are said to hunt at night, avoiding bright light. This creature was first spotted after the 1980 eruption of Mount St. Helens and is said to cause feelings of dread in those who cross its path. There are many theories to explain the Batsquatch's existence, including the idea that the volcano's violent eruption tore a hole in the fabric between two dimensions of space and the creature slipped into our world. The Batsquatch has been seen several times, most recently on April 14, 2014, when students in an Akron, Ohio high school spotted a giant black mass zip by a classroom window at incredible speed. The students described it as nine feet tall with a twenty-foot wingspan. In June 2011, a man was walking his dog when he saw something flying in the sky. He said it had had bat wings, blue fur, eyes glowing red and was about nine feet tall. In 2009 near California's Mount Shasta, several hikers witnessed a large, leather-winged creature fly out of a crevice in the mountain. At first, an eyewitness described the creature as having a head like a pterodactyl; however, on reconsideration, the witness claimed it was more akin to a flying fox bat. In April 1994, in Pierce County, Washington, adjacent to the cities of Olympia and Tacoma, another man described driving his truck when a large creature landed in front of him. He said it was human-like, nine feet tall with batlike wings and blue fur.

Chupacabra in Spanish means "goat-sucker," and the legend is believed to have originated in Puerto Rico, where the creature was first reported in 1995. It is said to predominantly roam there, in Mexico and the southwestern United States. The creature has been reported in the eastern United States and is known as the West Virginia Vampire for its blood-sucking ways. There have been reports of the creature in Oregon, including one 2019 incident in which five bulls were found mysteriously drained of blood. The chupacabra was said to have four legs, wide, dark eyes and three fingers. It was described as having spiky hair on its back and small air holes in place of a nose. It was also said to be a vampire-like creature that drained goats and other small animals of their blood. In the mid-2000s, the creature reemerged with stories of a hairless, coyote-like animal. When alleged chupacabra bodies were discovered, scientists tested their DNA, identifying them as normal animals that were affected by sarcoptic mange—their hair and fur had fallen out. However, mysteries and theories about the creature keep the legend alive to this day.

Ts'iichuk or Mosquito Folk are cryptids of the Pacific Northwest's Haida Native people. They are said to suck blood and other bodily fluids from their victims through a thorn-like proboscis in their mouths. One legend has that one of these creatures sucked the brain out of a baby that was being passed from adult to adult to admire and play with. The Ts'iichuk is somewhat like the creature known as a wraith, which has been featured in television programs like *Supernatural*, sucking the brains of the living through a spike or siphon in its wrist. The wraith appears human to the naked eye but casts a disfigured reflection in mirrors. Wraiths, like many monsters, can be beaten by using silver knives and other objects. Mosquito Folk are said to have once been human but were turned into their current form by their evil deeds. Like so many cryptids, these may be a cautionary tale reminding people to practice good deeds in life to avoid this horrible outcome.

This completes our time with Pacific Northwest cryptids. No doubt you'll agree Oregon and Washington have more than their fair share of these reported creatures, with close to forty.

6

LEGENDARY CURSES

Curses and Protections Against Them

The second area of Pacific Northwest legends and lore we'll focus on is curses. Psychologists sometimes refer to curses as "self-fulfilling prophecies," where belief in a curse produces belief in inevitable misfortune. Curses have existed almost as long as humans have inhabited the earth, with some examples being the King Tut's Curse (in which those who discovered his crypt were said to meet untimely deaths), the Hope Diamond curse (similarly, where owners of the diamond met untimely ends) and the Curse of Tippecanoe (in which Native Shawnee Tecumseh was said to have cursed future U.S. presidents elected twenty years apart in years ending in zero—the following died in office: William Henry Harrison, 1840; Abraham Lincoln, 1860; James A. Garfield, 1880; William McKinley, 1900; Warren G. Harding, 1920; Franklin D. Roosevelt, 1940; and John F. Kennedy, 1960). Curses on American sports teams include the 1945 Billy Goat Curse on the Chicago Cubs (they didn't win a World Series until 2016) and Babe Ruth's Bambino Curse on the Boston Red Sox (they didn't win a World Series until 2004) and others.

Curses and cursed items can be scary things. There are many superstitions about curses, including "don't think about the curse" or "don't look at or touch cursed objects," for fear you may fall victim to the curse. A curse is said to be created, in some cases, by a solemn invocation intended to employ a supernatural power to inflict harm or punishment on someone or something. The victim of the curse is thought to suffer devastating consequences. At a minimum, belief in curses can undermine confidence in oneself and in future success. Curses, like cryptids, have been the focus of movies and other popular media, including lighter fare such as Disney's 1991 *Beauty and the Beast* and 2004's *Ella Enchanted*, and the scary, such as 1973's *The Exorcist*.

There are said to be several ways to protect oneself against curses. These include taking a rosemary bath, doing a smoke cleansing (using sage, rosemary or mugwort); creating a protective salt barrier (which is like reported ways to protect oneself from ghosts); placing lemons on an altar; burning bay leaves, cinnamon and dragon's blood incense; and finally praying that the curse be ended. Some people, including mariners, believe certain tattoos on the body protect against curses. Other ways to protect against curses and hexes include creating a magic mirror that sends the curse back to the sender, creating a doll to absorb the damage in your place and meditating.

In addition to the human-created curses just described, there is another set of curses, or as the Bible's Book of Exodus calls them, "plagues," said to exist. These plagues feature prominently in the powerful 1923 and 1956 *Ten Commandments* movies, both by filmmaker Cecil B. DeMille. The ten plagues or natural disasters of Egypt, intended to force the Pharoah to let the Hebrew slaves leave Egypt, were turning water into blood, frogs, gnats, flies, a plague on livestock, boils, locusts, darkness, a plague on the Egyptians' firstborn and thunderstorms of hail and fire. It was that last curse or plague that may be analogous to several of the Pacific Northwest curses I describe here. Despite the Pacific Northwest's unmatched beauty and idyllic setting, there are several forms of natural phenomena that threaten the area: fires, earthquakes, tsunamis, volcanoes and violent storms. Some protective steps can be taken to deal with these events, such as strengthening buildings and other man-made structures against future earthquakes, but some of these natural events may be beyond humankind's ability to mitigate.

Like other supernatural and paranormal beliefs, believing in curses has helped Natives and others explain outcomes that may otherwise be difficult to explain. I discuss here several Pacific Northwest curses. Also in this section, I address several long-standing mysteries. Again, as elsewhere in this book, there are overlaps between what may be considered a curse as well as folklore.

The Pacific Northwest has no shortage of legendary curses.

ANDELANA AND STREETCAR DISASTERS

Andelana was a British four-masted barque, a large sailing ship. It docked in Tacoma, Washington's Commencement Bay on January 13, 1899. In my book *Haunted Puget Sound*, I discuss the ghosts attached to this event; here I focus on the reported curses.

Its crew thought the ship was unstable on the water, with unusually tall masts, and for this reason they wanted off the ship. Nine crew did successfully get off the ship in Tacoma, but the captain wouldn't allow the remaining seventeen to leave. Further, the captain had a photo taken of the remaining crew with their dogs to intimidate them, as if to say, "I know who you are— don't dare leave." Twenty-four hours later, all seventeen remaining crew were dead, having been trapped in their sleeping quarters when the ship sank. The *Andelana* was top-heavy, with no ballast to stabilize the ship as it awaited its shipment of wheat bound for Europe. A freak storm raced across Commencement Bay, with forty-mile-per-hour gusts, and capsized the ship in two hundred feet of water. A diver attempted to reach the *Andelana*, but the leather seal attaching his suit to oxygen ruptured, causing him to be crushed to death—the eighteenth human death related to this disaster. The *Andelana* has never been raised.

The next year, America's worst streetcar disaster took place on July 4, 1900. Tacoma Railway & Power Company's streetcar No. 55 malfunctioned, and riders awaited the next vehicle. At 8:00 a.m., Streetcar No. 116 pulled away from the stop in South Tacoma heading downtown. The Independence Day parade was forecasted to attract

Shipwreck, 1861. *Courtesy of Library of Congress, Alfred Waud artist.*

over 50,000 people. The streetcar was designed to hold 55 passengers, but about 150 people—some standing on the running boards, others hanging from the railings—crowded on board. The passengers weighed in at roughly fourteen thousand pounds or seven tons. Conditions were wet as the streetcar headed down a hill on Delin Street toward a sharp curve. Motorman F.L. Boehm, on the job less than a month, setting the electric engine in reverse, could not slow the overloaded vehicle. This was the fastest many of the passengers had ever traveled—this was prior to cars becoming common—as the streetcar traveled at fifty miles per hour instead of its usual ten. Passengers began to jump off, but many could not, as they were wedged into the vehicle. Where the track curved on to a trestle on C Street, now Commerce Street, close to the intersection with South Twenty-Sixth Street, the streetcar left the tracks, jumped a guardrail intended as a safety feature and plunged over one hundred feet into Gallagher's Gulch, now South Tacoma Way. The streetcar's ruptured steel and spraying glass caused catastrophic damage to riders. It landed upside down at the bottom of the ravine, with bodies of the dead either catapulted yards away or still stuck in the wreckage. Police officers, dressing for the parade, residents and those nearby heard the horrific crashing noise and attempted to provide aid to the victims. They described the scene as horrific, with 44 dead and over 70 seriously injured.

The following investigation and jury trial found the motorman responsible for allowing the streetcar to reach excessive speeds. They further found the company criminally negligent for assigning motorman Boehm an unfamiliar route and for improper maintenance of its cars, rails and the unsafe grade. Boehm testified he might have been able to safely negotiate the curve if the streetcar hadn't been overloaded. The company stopped using the trestle shortly thereafter, and it was torn down in 1910. By 1938, streetcars had been replaced by buses and other means of transportation.

The "curse" of the *Andelana* continued when someone chose to use bloodied wood from the Tacoma streetcar disaster to carve a model of the doomed ship. Some claim paranormal events have surrounded the model, with three individuals who encountered the model dying untimely deaths. Further, employees and visitors to Tacoma's Foss Seaport Museum, where I viewed the model—creepy!—claim their electronic devices have been "fried" when they got too close to the model, due to the supernatural energy produced by the cursed object. I must admit, I didn't get too close to the model and stood at a respectful distance while viewing it.

Another curse related to the Tacoma streetcar disaster resulted in the city's tearing up the streetcar tracks in 1939 and selling them as scrap to Japan—which was suffering raw material shortages due to its military operations in Asia—over the protests of Chinese Americans, who warned the steel would be turned into bombs and used against the United States. In fact, less than two years later, on December 7, 1941, the Japanese bombed Pearl Harbor, resulting in America's entry into World War II. No doubt the steel from Tacoma's streetcar tracks found its way into Japan's wartime weapons production.

ARTESIAN WELLS

At one time, there were one hundred artesian wells flowing in the city of Olympia, Washington's capital, that served as residents' primary source for water. Artesian water is that which flows naturally from underground to the surface and can be collected at wells. Olympia Beer was brewed in nearby Tumwater, Washington, from 1896 to 2003, and the factory still stands, vacant. The brewery's slogan was "It's the Water," referring to the artesian water with which the beer was brewed. There are two urban legends attached to Olympia's artesian wells: (1) the innocuous "if you drink from it, you'll come back to the city," and (2) the less innocuous and some would say curse, "if you drink from it, you'll die in Olympia and your resting place will be there."

The curse took a dark turn in 2013. A murder occurred in a homeless encampment on an embankment in Olympia along Interstate 5. A seventeen-year-old nicknamed "Sonic" was stabbed to death and his body burned inside a barrel. The police interrogated three other homeless nicknamed "Skitzo," "Red" and "Discord." The newspapers described this killing, including the homeless encampment's chaotic hierarchy and system of alliances, as the *Lord of the Flies* murder. This was in reference to the 1954 book and 1990 movie of the same name about boys who survive on an island after an airplane crash and their disastrous attempts at governing themselves. *Lord of the Flies* is also a Biblical reference, Matthew 12:22–28, to the devil and "darkness within." One of those accused of the murder, describing a dark reliance on the urban legend, inexplicably blamed the murder on the artesian water, saying, "If you drink the water—you'll never leave....It's the artesian well water, I blame it on that." I've talked with at least one Olympia resident who said she's never had Olympia tap water, rather drinking only artesian water—she was concerned when I mentioned the urban legends attached to the water.

BELLINGHAM CURSE

Today, Bellingham, Washington, is a beautiful, coastal, cool—attitude-wise—Pacific Northwest city of just under 100,000 near the Canadian border. But Bellingham wasn't always the laid-back city it is today. Several—the number is not clear—Chinese miners were killed (some say murdered) in 1876 in Bellingham Bay Coal Company's old Sehome coal mine under modern-day Bellingham. Sehome, first settled in 1853, was a small mining town and one of four early towns that combined in 1904 to form the city of Bellingham. Mining operations there ended in 1878 due in part to ships switching from burning coal to oil. The Chinese miners were said to have either been buried alive in the underground mine or drowned when it was filled with water, two years before the mine closed.

The Bellingham curse is the tale of the spirits of the dead miners cursing Bellingham's residents to be unable to leave the area or be destined to always return. In a 1949 article, the *Bellingham Herald* newspaper posed the question of whether the "ancestral ghosts of dead Chinese" haunted Bellingham. The article also quoted an unnamed "old-timer" miner who said the Chinese workers were not popular at the time of the mine disaster. I discuss the racism faced by Chinese communities in the Pacific Northwest in the next section on lore. Chinese laborers were accused of taking jobs from White workers and faced racism and expulsion from their homes and communities.

The Chinese workers were said to have gold in the money belts they were wearing when they were buried in the mine, fueling treasure hunting in the area—no gold has been found.

Later, in 1885, Chinese residents were expelled from Whatcom County, in which Bellingham is the largest city. Some came back, but they were restricted from White parts of towns such as Fairhaven, then a separate town, which later became part of Bellingham, by city ordinance and marked as the "Chinese Deadline." The deadline had a marker that made it clear Chinese were not allowed beyond that point from 1898 to 1903 under penalty of death. The Chinese worked at the world's biggest salmon cannery, and many in the White community wanted them kept out.

Truly a sad blemish on the history of the Pacific Northwest. Bellingham's mayor Dan Pike apologized in 2011, 108 years after the deadline, on behalf of the city for the wrongs heaped on the Chinese community. The apology is memorialized by a granite marker near a shoreline in Bellingham that replaced the deadline marker.

CAPE DISAPPOINTMENT

Cape Disappointment is a beautiful state park located in Ilwaco on Washington's coastal Long Beach Peninsula—where I used to live and lead tours. It was named in 1788 by British captain John Meares, who was searching for the entrance to the Columbia River but was left "disappointed" when he could not find it—in fact, he had but didn't realize it. This is what I refer to as "ground zero" for the treacherous and some say paranormal-laden Graveyard of the Pacific, which I discuss a little later. Some say Cape Disappointment is situated on cursed grounds and waters.

In 1853, three barques, large, three-masted sailing ships, sank there. One of those was the *Vandalia*, which sank on January 9, 1853. Four bodies washed ashore: Captain E.N. Beard, for whom Beards Hollow was named, and three other crew washed into what is now known as Deadmans Hollow. Prompted by the many shipwrecks, the U.S. government built navigational lights in the late 1850s. Two lighthouses were built at Cape Disappointment; one of them, named the North Head Lighthouse, went into service on May 16, 1898.

Life for lighthouse keepers was harsh. They had few visitors and kept a strict twenty-four-hour schedule, and the lighthouse is located at the second-windiest lighthouse site in the United States, with winds up to 120 miles per hour. In 1923, the lighthouse keeper was Alexander K. Pesonen, who lived there with his wife, Mary. Only twenty years old at the start, Mary endured this lonely, difficult life; remote location; and the howling winds for twenty-five years. In the spring of 1923, Mary saw her doctor in Portland, Oregon, who had diagnosed her with "melancholia, with persistent depression and ill-founded fears." Back home at the lighthouse, on June 8, Mary rose early and went for a walk with her dog Jerry. It was

North Head Lighthouse, Cape Disappointment, 2018. *Courtesy of Library of Congress, Carol M. Highsmith, photographer.*

reported that Jerry returned a short time later, acting strangely. A search party found Mary's coat lying on the edge of a cliff, 194 feet above the churning ocean. The tall grass leading to the cliff was disturbed, as if someone had slid down the cliff; Mary's body was retrieved from the rocks below. Mary had been a member of the Unity Movement, known for faith-based healings. A letter was discovered, which she reportedly wrote the night before her death, indicating she saw the error of her ways and prayed to God that she'd be able to do better even without her medicine. Her death occurred just six months before her husband's planned retirement. They had intended to buy a cranberry farm just a few miles away and spend their winters in California. Several newspapers reported on Mary's "rash act, illness, and temporary insanity," which caused "a troubled Mary to finally escape the harsh environment that had driven her mad." Mary's story is mirrored somewhat in the 2019 movie *The Lighthouse*, in which lighthouse keepers are driven to insanity by their arduous duty and isolation.

Beginning in the 1950s, staff and visitors have reported seeing Mary's ghost wandering through the lighthouse and the house where she and Alexander lived, appearing sad and distraught. In 2022, while leading tours of the area, I told this story. An elderly lady on the tour bus, made to look like an old-fashioned trolley, said she had visited the North Head Lighthouse as a child with her parents. She described climbing the spiral staircase, only to look up and see a woman in old-fashioned clothing staring down at her. She was scared to death, ran out of the lighthouse and has never returned.

I told her there is a photo of Mary Pesonen online, and I pulled it up on my phone and showed it to her. She responded, "That's the face I saw staring down at me!"

Chief Seattle's Curse

The great Suquamish and Duwamish Native Chief Seattle (1786–1866)—Chief Si'ahl in his Native language, for whom the city of Seattle is named—was known for his courage, leadership, battle skills, oratory abilities and pursuing a path of peaceful coexistence with White settlers. As a boy, in 1792, he watched British explorer George Vancouver's ships pass through Washington's Puget Sound. In the late eighteenth and early nineteenth centuries, Chief Seattle watched as his fellow Natives suffered through epidemics of smallpox, measles, influenza and other diseases carried by White settlers; tens of thousands died. Despite the suffering, he helped White settlers in times of distress. In one case, when there was a lack of milk for children, few if any cows existed in the area, he showed the settlers how to replace milk with clam juice. He also traded salmon, potatoes, venison and furs with the settlers.

Chief Seattle once accurately predicted "palefaces" would someday build "longhouses" or skyscrapers that stood on their sides and vertically reached toward the sky. He is also known for another prediction or, some would say, curse. On January 22, 1855, during the signing of the land settlement Treaty of Point Elliott between the Puget Sound Native tribes and the U.S. government, which called for all Duwamish Natives to relocate to reservations outside of Seattle, Chief Seattle described how the land was sacred to his people. He also said that when the last Native perished and the memory of the tribes was a myth, the invisible Native dead would swarm the White man's shores. This, the Chief said, would be particularly true at night when streets were deserted, and the Native dead would fill the empty streets, ensuring White residents were never alone. The chief's main message was that Whites should be just and deal fairly with the Native peoples because the Native dead would be present and watching.

Interestingly, one Native's spirit has been seen repeatedly at Pike Place Market in Seattle: Chief Seattle's eldest daughter, Princess Angeline, Kikisoblu in Lushootseed, who lived from 1820 to 1896. She lived in a small downtown shack by the waterfront and refused to leave Seattle, despite the

Treaty of Point Elliott. In 1856, during the Puget Sound War between Native tribes and the U.S. military, she conveyed a warning from her father to Seattle citizens about an imminent attack by a large Native force. The citizens were able to seek shelter during the Battle of Seattle and protect themselves. Her spirit, small in stature, bent and wrinkled wearing a red handkerchief over her head and a shawl, has been seen walking around the market near where she lived, slowly and painfully, and selling woven baskets. Is this a sign of Chief Seattle's prediction or curse coming true?

America does not have a good track record in its treatment of Native tribes.

EARTHQUAKES, TSUNAMIS, FIRES AND VOLCANOES

The Pacific Northwest has seen more than its fair share of natural disasters. If those of us who live in this wonderful part of America are blessed with its natural beauty, we are also threatened with the many natural and man-made disasters that have befallen us and will again.

The Pacific Northwest faces the threat of earthquakes from subduction zone megathrusts, shallow crustal faults and deep intraplate faults. Several earthquakes struck the region in the twentieth century, with lives lost and many buildings destroyed. The last megathrust earthquake was on January 26, 1700, and scientists say these occur in four to six hundred intervals; we are overdue for an overwhelming earthquake with a potential 9-plus on the Richter Scale. Because of the Pacific Northwest's location by the Pacific Ocean, the region is also in danger of giant waves or tsunamis. The last major tsunami in the region accompanied the 1700 earthquake. The accounts we have of these events were from Chinook, Hoh, Quileute, Tillamook and other Natives of present-day Oregon and Washington. They described it in supernatural terms, as a terrible fight between Thunderbird and Whale, with mountain dwarfs striking their earthquake drums, shaking the mountains, uprooting trees and covering the earth with ocean water. Scientists say the coast dropped as much as 6.5 feet with floods 984 feet inland, creating still existing "ghost forests" of dead trees, killed by the salt water. Whole villages were swallowed, and many lives lost. Over the next fifty years, the chance of another 9.0 earthquake is one in ten. We have seismic networks and tsunami warnings systems, but we are still not fully prepared. Even "earthquake-proof" buildings were built with short-sharp California-type quakes in

Horse-drawn fire engine, 2024. *Courtesy of Jason McLean.*

mind, not the Pacific Northwest's stronger, longer ones. We have little choice but to remain vigilant, knowing we may have less than thirty minutes warning in the case of tsunamis and no warning at all before catastrophic earthquakes.

Fire has struck and destroyed many of the area's great cities and towns. One example was Portland, Oregon's Great Fire of 1873. Twenty-two blocks of the city, including over two hundred dwellings and hundreds of stores, were destroyed, with losses topping $25 million in today's dollars. The fire stopped only when it ran out of material to burn. The Great Seattle Fire of 1889 caused millions of dollars in property damage and destroyed the entire twenty-five-block downtown area. Surprisingly, while the fire itself claimed only a few lives, dozens of workers lost their lives in the subsequent cleanup of the city. Fires in the Pacific Northwest, and elsewhere, were not uncommon in the late nineteenth century. Sidewalks and streets were made of wood—often planks on top of logs, as were most buildings—this was thought to be an advance over earlier dirt paths and roads. Further, fire departments were run more like private clubs, paid for by business owners, with inadequate organization and resources.

Finally, the Pacific Northwest's Cascade Mountain Range has many volcanoes, including the 14,411-foot-tall Mount Rainier. Many of us remember Washington's Mount St. Helens eruption on Mary 18, 1980: fifty-seven people were killed, hundreds of square miles were turned into wasteland, tens of thousands of animals were killed, and losses totaled over $1 billion. We can educate ourselves on where volcano impacts, such as lahars—violent mud flows—may strike, the hazard maps and evacuation routes. We should also have ways to stay informed, keep in touch and have supplies to survive while awaiting help.

Other parts of America face weather-related threats—floods, hurricanes, snowstorms, tornados—but the Pacific Northwest faces many that are unique to this part of the country. It does seem we are both blessed and cursed.

JAKE BIRD HEX

Tacoma, Washington's vacant Old City Hall was built in 1893 and served as the city's government headquarters for fifty years. The building has been largely vacant since the 1950s. Criminals were housed in the building's jail at the turn of the twentieth century. The most famous prisoner was Jake Bird, who was captured after hacking two people to death in 1947 with an axe and confessed to killing forty-four people. It is said that Bird, at the end of his trial, placed a curse on those who captured, jailed and sentenced him. He said that those involved would die before he did, and it's said that six of those individuals died before Bird was put to death two years later. The curse is known as the Jake Bird Hex. It's also common for the bell in the Old City Hall's clock tower to ring unexpectedly and without apparent explanation late at night or early in the morning, even though the building is empty. Police have investigated the unexplained bell ringing but found no evidence of the living being responsible.

LEWIS AND CLARK'S CHALLENGES, THE MYSTERIES OF MERIWETHER LEWIS AND SACAGAWEA

After America's Louisiana Purchase from France in 1803, which today accounts for about one-third of the United States, President Thomas Jefferson wished to explore the newly purchased territory and the land beyond the "great rock mountains" to the west. He commissioned explorers William Clark and Meriwether Lewis, along with their Corps of Discovery, to explore the West and Pacific Northwest in 1804–6. Lewis had served as Jefferson's private secretary, and Clark had previously served as Lewis's superior officer in the U.S. Army. Lewis and Clark were good friends, and although Lewis, a captain, outranked Clark, a lieutenant, he insisted they serve as co-captains of the expedition. Few if any individuals did more to contribute to the scientific and geographic knowledge of the Pacific Northwest than Lewis and Clark. Their exploration gave rise to industry, with the fur trade one of the earliest examples, and strengthened America's interest in and claims of what would become the West Coast. It also, unfortunately, led to the widespread displacement of Native tribes from their homes onto reservations.

In these times of paved roads, air travel, GPS and other technologies, it isn't possible to overstate the hardships Lewis and Clark faced in their travels. President Jefferson believed the group might encounter dinosaurs, mountains of salt, Welsh-speaking Natives, herds of wooly mammoths and giant ground sloths. While they didn't encounter any long-extinct animals, they did encounter mountains of salt in present-day Utah, and the Mandan Native tribe, which appeared to speak a language related to Welsh; it's thought this was due to Welsh explorers intermarrying with the Natives. They also documented 122 new animal species, including the grizzly bear, coyote and a mysterious, giant bird that was most likely a California condor. They also faced harsh weather, dangerous waters, disease, starvation, strange terrain, unknown wildlife and friendly as well as hostile Natives. The Corps was ready for challenges from European powers, Natives and others, carrying one of the largest arsenals of that time, west of the Mississippi, including tomahawks, pikes, knives, rifles (including an experimental air rifle) and muskets; two hundred pounds of gunpower; and four hundred pounds of lead for making bullets. Famously helping the Corps on their journey was Sacagawea, a teenage Shoshone Native who was both a wife and slave, having been purchased by her husband, Toussaint Charbonneau. She served as an interpreter and guide for the group and in 1805 protected them in an encounter with other Shoshones whose tribe's chief turned out to be her long-lost brother—referred to as the "Shoshone Miracle."

Spain sent one thousand soldiers to arrest the Corps' members but fortunately were unsuccessful in locating them. Lewis was almost killed in an encounter with a grizzly bear, and the Corps came across at least forty bears on their journey. Despite the hardships, only one member of the Corps died during the journey: Sergeant Charles Floyd died in 1804 due to what was most likely a burst appendix. On October 29, 1805, while sailing down the Columbia River in present-day Oregon, Lewis and Clark passed several islands on which local Native Chinook tribes placed their dead, wrapped in robes, mats or furs and left in canoes in and leaning against trees. The Natives considered these to be sacred "islands of the dead" and called them Memaloose, based on the Chinook word *memalust*, meaning "to die." The Corps called one of these islands Sepulcher Island, meaning "burial island." Those burial grounds were later desecrated by White settlers, from the 1880s until the 1930s, and the remains disturbed.

It seemed to rain most days during their exploration near present-day Astoria, Oregon, in late 1805 and 1806; their clothes rotted off their backs. On November 10, 1805, facing driving rain, strong winds and high waves, the Corps members dragged their canoes into a small notch on the shoreline they called Dismal Nitch. They were stranded there for five days, finally moving forward on November 15. The Corps made it around Point Distress, landing and setting up a survey headquarters on a sandy beach on the north side of the Columbia River, east of modern-day Chinook, Washington, at a location later called Station Camp. This was also the site of a major Chinook Native village called Middle Village. During the 2022 history and haunted tours I led of the region, we always stopped at the site of Station Camp and Middle Village where there are Native canoes and story boards telling of the historic importance of the site.

On March 23, 1806, the Corps, having finished their work in the Pacific Northwest, headed for St. Louis and home. The group split in two near what is today Lolo, Idaho, to thoroughly explore on their way back. Although most encounters with Natives had been positive, Lewis's group was attacked by Blackfoot Natives, two of whom were killed while trying to steal guns. On August 11, 1806, on their return journey east, private Pierre Cruzatte, who was partially blind, shot Lewis in the thigh after mistaking him for an elk—Lewis was wearing elk skins. On September 21, 1806, the reunited Corps reached St. Charles in present-day Missouri.

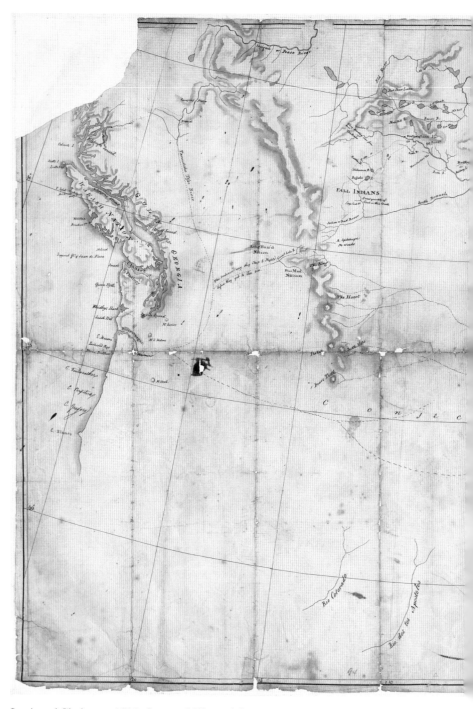

Lewis and Clark map, 1803. *Courtesy of Library of Congress*.

Corps members fired their weapons into the air, marking their arrival. Townspeople exuberantly welcomed them in great surprise, as many had thought the expedition members had perished on their journey. On September 23, 1806, the Corps reached St. Louis, which caused a national sensation as, again, many thought they were dead. Lewis and Clark were seen as national heroes, having braved the dangers of the unknown and succeeding in mapping America's new lands. Separately, a former Corps member, explorer John Colter, was the first White man to visit in 1807 what would become Yellowstone National Park. He described water shooting straight up out of the ground at great velocity—what would become Old Faithful—and other thermal wonders, but these seemingly outlandish claims were not readily believed. I visited Yellowstone in September 2023, and the natural wonders are incredible.

Clark enjoyed great success after the expedition, being appointed brigadier general and superintendent of Indian affairs for the Territory of Upper Louisiana. Subsequently, in 1813, he was made Missouri Territory governor, which he remained until 1820. Clark was seen as a leading expert on the West, consulted by six presidents through the Van Buren administration. He died in 1838 at age sixty-eight in the home of his firstborn son, Meriwether Lewis Clark.

Sacagawea, longing to revisit her former "native country," never achieved this, seemingly dying at about age twenty-five in 1812 from "putrid fever" near current-day Bismarck, North Dakota. We believe this in part because fur trader John Luttig's journal noted "the wife of Charbonneau …died." Further indicating her death, William Clark became guardian to Sacagawea's two children, seven-year-old Jean Baptiste and four-month-old Lisette, with his paying for Baptiste's education. Lisette's fate is unknown. However, whether Sacagawea died in 1812 has been questioned, as she was not Charbonneau's only wife. Also, Native oral history says Sacagawea left her husband, moved west, returned to the Shoshone in Wyoming and remained there until her death in 1884, when she would have been in her nineties. We may never know for sure!

Shortly after Lewis's return in March 1807, President Jefferson appointed him governor of the newly acquired Louisiana Territory. Strangely, Lewis waited a year before going to St. Louis to begin his new duties. Once he arrived, Lewis incurred debt by buying properties, and allegations were made about Lewis's handling of government funds. Also, despite Lewis's requests, the new James Madison administration refused to reimburse him for expenses he incurred. In August 1809, a distraught Lewis wrote to officials in Washington of his innocence and asked for a fair investigation. In the early fall of 1809, Lewis headed to Washington, D.C., from St. Louis to clear his name. It is said he was severely depressed; someone who encountered him on his journey described him as having "mental derangement." Further, he twice attempted suicide on his trip. On October 10, 1809, thirty-five-year-old Lewis stayed at the Grinder's Stand Inn near Hohenwald, Tennessee. Mrs. Grinder observed Lewis "pacing and mumbling in a strange manner," which she said scared her, and she kept her distance. Later that night, after Lewis had gone to bed, it is said that Mrs. Grinder was awakened by two gunshots, and through a crack in her bedroom door, she saw Lewis stagger and fall, followed by him exclaiming, "Oh, Lord," as he crawled down the hall. Mrs. Grinder inexplicably didn't summon Lewis's servants until two hours after he was shot. They discovered him lying on a blood-soaked robe, with gunshot wounds to his chest and head. Lewis told them he was "no coward, but was strong," and said it was "so hard to die." It was reported Lewis had shot himself with two guns, and both former President Thomas Jefferson and his co-captain William Clark believed it was suicide. This was thought based on his depression, financial situation, the challenges of his governorship, drinking and his lack of a love life—he described himself as a "fusty, musty, rusty old bachelor… void in our hearts." However, Lewis's relatives believed he was murdered by his free Creole servant John Pernier, whom he owed wages and with whom he was traveling. Further, there were bandits reported nearby at the time of his death. Finally, the two gun shots, one to the chest and the other to his head, and his crawling before dying, cast some doubt on whether it was a suicide. He was buried on the inn's property, which is part of today's Meriwether Lewis State Park and is commemorated by the Meriwether Lewis National Monument. The historic marker mentions the controversy surrounding Lewis's death: "Life of romantic endeavor and lasting achievement came tragically and mysteriously to its close." Lewis's debts were paid by the Madison administration two years after his death.

To this day, it is unclear if Lewis's death was a suicide; he battled depression, mood swings and heavy drinking most of his life and was reported to have previously attempted suicide. But suicides do not usually involve two gunshots. Lewis's mysterious death has been the subject of books and movies, including the 2022 movie *Mysterious Circumstance: The Death of Meriweather Lewis*. Visitors to the monument—as well as visitors to Lewis statues, which are numerous throughout the Pacific Northwest, including at the massive Joint Base Lewis-McChord in southern Washington—have reported feeling a restless energy and a strange unseen force. Visitors have also reported hearing metal, like a water scoop, scraping an empty bucket, as well as the words "so hard to die."

Maltby's Thirteen Steps to Hell

Maltby Cemetery near Bothell, Washington, in use from 1905 to 1967, is said to hold a secret and a curse. There are thirteen stairs leading to the tomb of a local wealthy family. One legend has it that when someone walked down the stairs, all was quiet until they reached the bottom, where they collapsed and experienced visions of hell, including fiery chambers. Another legend is that the person walking down the stairs disappeared to those up above, only to reappear many miles away. A third legend is teenagers, dared by their friends to walk down the stairs, went into a catatonic state and were unable to speak upon exiting the

Cemetery, 2024. *Courtesy of Jason McLean.*

tomb. Apparitions of women and children in tattered clothing have also been seen. Some visitors reported no flowers nearby on entering but spotting fresh flowers placed on tombstones on exiting. The thirteen steps are said to no longer be accessible, located on private property and at least partially covered over. Like some curses and urban legends, this story may exist in part to dissuade teenagers and others from disturbing this cemetery.

Marcus Whitman

In the entry lobby of the Washington State Capitol in Olympia, built in 1928, is a statue of Marcus Whitman. Paranormal researchers have set up their EVP (electronic voice phenomenon) and other equipment in the capitol, recording disembodied voices and other supernatural evidence. Whitman was the first medical doctor west of the Rocky Mountains and was a leader of the Oregon Trail's first wagon train. This sculpture is one of three that were created. One was sent to the U.S. Capitol in Washington, D.C. Each state can submit two statues to the Capitol's statuary hall; that statue was removed in 2021 due to the controversial nature of Marcus Whitman, explained in a moment, and replaced with a statue of Native activist Billy Frank Jr. Whitman and his wife, Narcissa, were medical missionaries, ministering to the Natives of easternmost Washington State in the 1830s. A measles outbreak hit that part of Washington and decimated Native children—as mentioned, in some parts of the Pacific Northwest, 90 percent of Native populations were destroyed by diseases carried by White settlers. White children were also struck by the measles epidemic but were affected to a far lesser degree. The Natives blamed Whitman, his wife and other missionaries and massacred thirteen of them in November 1847. This launched the Cayuse War between Natives and the U.S. military, which lasted for seven years, with a great loss of life. Five Natives were hanged in 1847 for the massacre. One other copy of the Whitman statue stands at Whitman College in Walla Walla, Washington—named for Marcus Whitman, as is Whitman County in eastern Washington. It too has been controversial and vandalized repeatedly, although it has not been removed. The statue in Olympia shares in the controversy, but efforts to have it replaced have failed to date. In addition to the bad blood, if not a curse, caused by

Marcus Whitman
statue, 2018.
*Courtesy of Library
of Congress, Carol
M. Highsmith,
photographer.*

these statues, there are haunted paranormal stories around the Cayuse
battlefields near Walla Walla. Visitors have reported hearing the beating
of horse hooves into the ground, as if the battles are still taking place—no
horses are present.

NATIVE DEATH CULTURE

A Native ghost or death cult on the Columbia River and in other Pacific
Northwest locations was said to exist in the nineteenth century. It is thought
that this cult was formed in reaction to the incursion of White people, and
as mentioned, the resulting deaths of about 90 percent of the Chinook
Natives and other coastal peoples, killed between the 1770s and 1850.
Along with other coastal tribes, the Chinook were killed, in part, due to
diseases such as smallpox, malaria and measles. White settlers also overran
and stole Native lands in search of fur, gold and opportunity. The flooding
of Native American villages and the displacement of burial grounds, as

the U.S. government built the Bonneville (1938), Grand Coulee (1942) and other dams, could be seen as another step in the destruction of the Native cultures along the Columbia River.

Bone carvings of human and animal figures with prominent rib cages were discovered in old burial pits, figures that the Natives believed represented death. Anthropologists have indicated there was an old Native belief in the impending destruction and renewal of the world—a belief that seemed to be confirmed by the tragic way and speed in which the Natives of the Lower Columbia Valley, the Oregon and Washington coasts and along the Columbia River disappeared. The Natives believed they were cursed, largely by the presence and incursion of White settlers.

NAUTICAL SUPERSTITIONS

Oregon has close to 400 miles of shoreline, while Washington has 3,026 miles, including Puget Sound and other inlets. Therefore, it isn't surprising that nautical superstitions, including curses, have helped shape the Pacific Northwest's history and folklore. When discussing nautical superstitions, I would be remiss if I didn't mention the fact that mariners, in general, were a superstitious lot and believed in curses of various types. The reported nautical paranormal activity associated with Pacific Northwest lighthouses, pirates, shipwrecks, etc., is heavily influenced by seafaring legacies and accompanying superstitions.

Many nautical superstitions are reflected in Herman Melville's 1851 novel *Moby-Dick* and the 1956 movie of the same name. Melville wrote the book while living in his home, Arrowhead, in my hometown of Pittsfield, Massachusetts. One fatalistic nineteenth-century belief among sailors was that "what the sea wants, the sea will have." This was because many sailors could not swim, and even bathing in the ocean was considered dangerous. In the seafaring realm, it's considered unlucky to begin a voyage on a Friday because Jesus was crucified on a Friday. Seeing a person with red hair, who is cross-eyed, or flat-footed was thought to be bad luck. A woman onboard was believed to anger the sea gods, who might send violent storms. Flowers, ministers and ringing bells, other than those rung purposely by the crew, are thought to be for funerals and, thus, forecast death and bad luck. If someone's sweetheart brought flowers aboard, the flowers were thrown overboard—again, because flowers are used for funerals. Killing a gull, albatross or dolphin brought bad luck, as did stepping aboard with your left foot, losing a bucket overboard or seeing rats running off the ship. The adage that sailors should take caution when there is a red sky in the morning, whereas a red sky at night should provide comfort, is thought to have some basis in fact. If the air is clear, sunset is said to be tinted red. But red light in the morning may mean moisture is in the air, thus increasing the likelihood of stormy weather. Clapping hands aboard a ship and the presence of umbrellas were thought to tempt thunder and foul weather. Throwing stones into the ocean was thought to cause storms and huge swells. Strange sounds heard

Man with nautical equipment, 1903. *Courtesy of Library of Congress, Detroit Publishing Co.*

while at sea were often blamed on sirens or mermaids whose songs could lure sailors to their deaths. The sight of a bare-breasted woman was thought to calm an angry sea; hence ships' wooden "figureheads" were often carved on the front or bow of the ship in the form of bare-breasted, well-endowed women. A ship's name ending in the letter -*a* was considered unlucky, and some would say the *Lusitania* and the *Britannia* proved this point when they were sunk by German torpedoes. Other seafaring superstitions include never painting your ship green, as doing so will cause the vessel to beach itself in a gale. Turning a cup or bucket upside down will cause the boat to overturn. Whistling in the wheelhouse will cause high winds. Always batten down the hatches and never leave a hatch cover lying upside down. When heading to the ship, one should never turn back, and saying the word *pig* was to be avoided at all costs.

I keep these superstitions in mind when I boarded and rode the old-fashioned schooner from which I led history and folklore tours, as well as when I'm serving as an onboard historian on cruise ships and travel by cruise ship while on vacation. Many at-sea calamities are said to be linked to the violation of these superstitions. Like so much folklore, these superstitions may be in response to other difficult-to-explain calamities at sea. Related to both mariners' superstitions and curses, many sailors historically have had tattoos—based on the Polynesian word *tattow*,

Deep-sea diver, 2024. *Courtesy of Jason McLean.*

documented by British captain James Cook in 1769—engraved on their bodies. These, in part, are intended to ward off curses, especially if they are in the shape of crosses, hearts or flowers. They are thought to act as good-luck charms.

OAKVILLE BLOBS

On August 7, 1994, and on five other occasions over the next three weeks, gelatinous blobs fell like rain or hail on the small town of Oakville, Washington—population six hundred at the time—in between Olympia and Aberdeen in Grays Harbor County and the surrounding area. The material was later labeled "Oakville Blobs," and each was the size of a grain of rice, like translucent gelatin. Local police and residents were dumbfounded by what this strange substance could have been, and these events were reported in the national news, including the *New York Times*, and covered in episodes of *Unsolved Mysteries* and *Monsters and Mysteries in America*.

The day the blobs first occurred, residents began getting sick with flu-like symptoms, including shortness of breath and ear infections. Dozens of people were hospitalized, and small animals died. One of the ill residents' daughters sent a sample of the blobs to the Washington State Department of Ecology Hazardous Material Unit. Microbiologists found two species of bacteria in the blobs: *Pseudomonas flourescens*, which can be harmful to people with immune system troubles, and *Enterobacter collacae*, which can contribute to lung, blood and urinary and digestive tract infections.

No samples were maintained of the blobs, and to this day it is not clear what they were. Some believe they were parts of jellyfish dispersed into rain clouds by U.S. military bombing exercises fifty miles away over the Pacific Ocean. Others believed it may have been fluid waste from an airliner lavatory, but the U.S. Federal Aviation Administration indicated such material would be blue and not translucent like the blobs. Interestingly, such gelatinous, translucent blobs have been reported since the fourteenth century, labeled "star jelly" or "astral jelly," and known to fall during meteor showers. In some ways, the Oakville Blobs appeared to some to be like the biblical curses that played out in Exodus, described earlier. Strange!

OLD MAN OF THE LAKE AND THE SPIRITS OF WIZARD ISLAND

Crater Lake in south-central Oregon is the deepest lake in the United States, at just under two thousand feet deep. It was created six thousand years ago when the nearby volcano Mount Mazama erupted and collapsed. The melting snow, along with rain, created the lake in the resulting crater.

Crater Lake, 1942.
Courtesy of Library of Congress, Lee Russell photographer.

Klamath Natives believed the lake to be cursed and inhabited by evil spirits. There are two islands there: Wizard Island (a volcanic cinder cone) and Phantom Ship (thought to resemble a ship). A tree stump dating to 1896 protruding vertically out of Crater Lake is nicknamed the "Old Man of the Lake." There are stories that the Old Man can control the weather, as evidenced in 1988 when the stump was tied down to allow submarine exploration of the lake. Suddenly, the weather turned from clear to stormy, and it is reported to have snowed in August. Once the stump was released, the weather went back to clear. Wizard Island appears to be floating in the middle of the lake and is in the shape of a wizard's hat. There are age-old stories of ghostly campfires on the island, and when rangers go to investigate, they find no evidence of fires. One person reported a roaring bonfire with ten people standing around it, but no evidence of the fire or people was ever found. Natives believed the lake to be cursed, with hexes placed on the water. One Native tale tells the story of two spirits, named Llao and Skell, who were said to have battled at Crater Lake. Both died, and they continue to haunt the surrounding area, causing massive storms.

OREGON'S CENTRAL COAST

Oregon's coast, as well as Washington's, is stunningly beautiful. It is difficult to imagine a more beautiful setting than Newport in the south to Cannon

Beach, in the north of Oregon, where giant rocky outcroppings meet the Pacific Ocean. Despite this idyllic setting, some people believe and there are long-standing stories of the coast being cursed. In part, this curse is because the area is in the Graveyard of the Pacific—mentioned elsewhere—and where over two thousand ships and countless lives have been lost due to the dangerous waters, shipwrecks, storms, sandbars and other reasons primarily in the late nineteenth and early twentieth centuries. Another reason is the staggering loss of life suffered by the Chinook, Clatsop and other Native tribes. Further, the coastal highways are said to run through and on top of old Native burial grounds, which some believe to be haunted. Building on top of Native burial grounds, especially when the bodies have not been moved, is a regular "haunted" theme in books and movies. One example is 1982's Steven Spielberg movie *Poltergeist*, in which the dead came to life after a housing complex was built on top of a Native burial ground. People have heard strange noises along the Oregon coast, including in the forests, which are said to not sound natural. Couple these factors with other purportedly paranormal occurrences, including some covered elsewhere in this book— Bandage Man, Bigfoot, Fort Stevens, pirates, the Terrible Tilly lighthouse and others—and it's not difficult to imagine why some believe the central Oregon coast is cursed.

Oregon coast, 2000. *Courtesy of Library of Congress, Carol M. Highsmith, photographer.*

PACIFIC COUNTY REPRESENTATIVES

On what is now a vacant parking lot on Capitol Way in the historic district of downtown Olympia, Washington, stood the two-story building where the Washington Territorial Legislature met in 1854. Washington had been broken off from the larger Oregon Territory in 1853, with Olympia made the new capital. Earlier, in 1846, Great Britain and the United States created the new international border at the forty-ninth parallel. Olympia became the new capital because it had served as a "port of entry" for the Oregon Territory on the waters of Puget Sound, it sat in the middle of the territory and there was long-standing U.S. political presence there. Each Washington county sent representatives to serve in the new legislature. Pacific County on the Washington coast, where I formerly lived, sent three representatives in succession. Unfortunately, a curse appeared to claim the first three representatives sent by this county. The first, J.L. Brown, died on the arduous two-day trip to Olympia through the woods and over water—today that trip is two and a half hours by car. The second, Jehu Scudder, also died en route. The third, Henry Fiester, made it, attended a meeting, went to a bar with fellow legislators and then fell off the barstool, dead, cause unknown. James Strong, the fourth Pacific County representative, made it and was seated. It certainly appears the representatives Pacific County sent were cursed; no other county suffered the loss of their representatives in this way. These events also reflect the dangerous and arduous travel conditions in Washington and the greater Pacific Northwest in the mid- to late nineteenth century, due to the thick and mountainous forests, dangerous waters, weather and fog, all at a time before roads were built in the early twentieth century.

SEATTLE WINDSHIELD PITTING DELUSION

In March 1954, people in Bellingham, Washington, north of Seattle, started noticing small pockmarks in their car windshields. Some thought the damage was due to items ranging from sand fleas to atomic bomb testing fallout. In April of that year, Seattle residents began noticing similar damage to their windshields. Like the Oakville Blobs, mentioned earlier, it appeared to some to be like the biblical curses that played out in Exodus. President Dwight D. Eisenhower, Washington's governor and research scientists were notified of these strange and concerning events.

A 1950s car, 2018.
Courtesy of Library
of Congress, Carol M.
Highsmith, photographer.

The pockmark events spread to other states and Canada and damaged airplane cockpits and greenhouse roofs. This may sound silly to us, some seventy years later, but at the time, these events caused a near-hysterical reaction. By the end of the summer of 1954, the "pit mania" had begun to dissipate, but definitive answers were never found. It's thought that maybe the pockmarks were just the normal wear and tear on windows, and without media attention, these concerns go away on their own.

SLAVERY

Some may think American Civil War–era slavery, a curse that has haunted America for much of its history, occurred only in the American South or Confederacy and certainly not in the Pacific Northwest. However, at least in one case, it did occur here, and it was the only recorded instance of an enslaved person escaping from bondage in the Washington Territory.

In 1855, new Washington territorial surveyor General James Tilton arrived from Maryland, a border state, on the Union-Confederacy border, which allowed slavery. He had with him an eight-year-old Black slave named Charles Mitchell, born in 1847 at Marengo Plantation on Chesapeake Bay, Talbot County, Maryland. In 1857, the U.S. Supreme Court upheld chattel slavery in the territories with its Dred Scott decision. Based on this, Mitchell remained Tilton's slave, even though both were in the Washington Territory.

In what has been described as the Maritime Underground Railroad, harkening to the legendary Underground Railroad used to smuggle the enslaved out of the American South, on September 24, 1860, Mitchell was smuggled out of Olympia, Washington, on board the *Eliza Anderson* sidewheeler to Victoria, Canada. Mitchell was caught by the ship's captain and first officer on behalf of Tilton. However, when the ship arrived in Victoria, it was met by a writ of habeas corpus, an action protecting against unlawful and indefinite imprisonment, demanding Mitchell be freed. In what became an international incident. the men holding Mitchell turned him over to Canadian authorities and he was freed.

In June 1862, Congress outlawed slavery in the territories and President Lincoln signed it into law. Charles Mitchell was lost to history, and his movements following the incidents in Washington and Canada are unknown.

TERRIBLE TILLY LIGHTHOUSE

In 1878, the U.S. government decided a lighthouse was needed to guide ships around Tillamook Head, just northwest of Cannon Beach, Oregon, as perilous weather and geography made seafaring dangerous. Congress allocated $50,000, equivalent to $1.3 million in 2020, for its construction. The head is a 1,200-foot-high, 15-million-year-old steep, rocky bluff jutting out of the ocean. The Tillamook Rock Lighthouse was to be built on the head, but as the head was frequently shrouded in fog, the lighthouse was, instead, built on a large piece of basalt rock located a mile offshore, known simply as the "Rock." Despite its innocuous appearance, the lighthouse quickly became known as Terrible Tilly for the strong storms, arduous working conditions, ghostly legends, mysteries and myths surrounding it.

Members of the Native Tillamook tribe warned the lighthouse builders that the basalt rock location was cursed by their gods and haunted by evil spirits; the Tillamook avoided it. Tragedy struck almost immediately. On September 18, 1879, the curse was experienced as master mason John R. Trewavas, the first surveyor of the location, lost his footing and was swept out to sea; his remains were never found. Knowing the difficulties of the location, locals refused to work on the lighthouse's construction. A new surveyor, Charles A. Ballantyne, was appointed and had to hire a construction crew from outside the area. The crew was housed at Cape Disappointment to ensure locals would not scare them away.

Terrible Tilly Lighthouse. *Courtesy of Pixabay, chrisnjule.*

Constructing the lighthouse was no easy feat. On January 2, 1880, a terrible storm struck the Rock. Provisions and tools were swept away by enormous waves, and the nine lighthouse construction workers hunkered down as best they could. Sixteen days after the storm hit, despite rumors of their demise, the workers were found in good health but in great need of food and supplies. On January 3, 1881, with the lighthouse close to completion but not yet lit, a second instance of the curse occurred. The 1,200-ton British ship *Lupatia* wrecked on the Rock. It had been caught in strong winds and heavy fog, causing poor visibility. The lighthouse construction crew heard shouts of "hard aport," masts and rigging creaking and saw faint lights as the ship struggled to avoid the Rock. The *Lupatia* sank, killing all sixteen crew members on board. Twelve bodies washed ashore, while the other four were never found. The only survivor was the crew's Australian shepherd puppy. After 575 days of construction, and at a cost of $123,493, equivalent to $3.1 million in 2020, the lighthouse went into operation on January 21, 1881. Four lightkeepers at a time were assigned to work the light; they were responsible for maintaining the light, which guided ships through the treacherous waters.

Since operations began, tales of paranormal occurrences have surrounded Terrible Tilly. James A. Gibbs served at the lighthouse from 1945 to 1946.

Gibbs was a prolific author of books about the Pacific Northwest, including *Tillamook Light* about Terrible Tilly, *Pacific Graveyard* and others. Gibbs said he had been warned by the three other lighthouse keepers that ghosts inhabited the lighthouse. Gibbs reported hearing disembodied footsteps, the feeling of air brushing by his throat and the sounds of moaning. Gibbs also said that he and the other lightkeepers once saw an eerie, lifeless ghost ship drifting aimlessly near the rocks, only to turn around and head back to sea. The lighthouse keepers reported the incident to the U.S. Coast Guard, but no ship could be identified. Other stories include the spirit of a former lighthouse keeper said to be a malevolent poltergeist, a German word meaning "noisy ghost," and thought capable of chasing, attacking and hurting people. A benevolent spirit is also said to haunt the lighthouse: the ghost of a lighthouse keeper who wanted to be—and was—buried on the lighthouse grounds.

On September 1, 1957, the lighthouse was deactivated, made obsolete by new technology. Strangely fitting, from 1980 to 1999, Terrible Tilly was used as a columbarium, storing urns with cremated human remains.

This concludes our discussion of Pacific Northwest legendary curses, many of which are head-scratching. Next, we'll talk more about the folklore of the Pacific Northwest.

7

LORE

Folklore, Superstitions and Urban Legends

The third area of Pacific Northwest legends and lore we'll discuss relates to other areas of folklore unrelated to cryptids and curses. Folklore literally means the lore of the folk or people. *Lore* means "knowledge," so a fair translation would be "folk knowledge." When I say *knowledge*, I mean the accepted, conventional wisdom of a society that is taken for granted as being true. Folklore includes the traditional knowledge that is passed on from generation to generation. Folklore or lore has a rich history, and all legends have an origin story. In many cases, tales were created by rural, frequently poor, peasants and others, through which they expressed a shared identity by way of traditional stories. Folklore takes many forms, including material (art, architecture, textiles, musical, narrative), legends, fairy tales and verbal (jokes and proverbs). Englishman William Thoms coined the term *folklore* in 1846 and used the phrase to replace the words *popular antiquities* and *popular literature*. It differs from history, which is made up of past events and changes in society. It is thought that folklore gives us the wisdom to understand history from a different point of view. Folklore showcases humankind's problems and successes. While much of folklore plays a positive role in a society's culture, enhancing a sense of history and commonality, some folklore—such as the German Nazis' belief in their superiority—has a negative effect. The Pacific Northwest has no shortage of folkloric tales, especially dark ones; I describe many of them here.

Folklore includes imaginative tales that cover a wide range of topics: romantic encounters, origins of popular holidays and lighthearted fables. Lighthearted American fables include Paul Bunyan, the giant woodsman who, with his blue ox, Babe, created major landmarks, including Washington's Puget Sound; John Henry, the famed railroad builder; Johnny Appleseed, the scatterer of apple seeds; and Davy Crockett, the pioneer who died fighting for Texas's independence from Mexico at the Alamo. In this book, instead of those lighthearted fables, I examine the darker side of folklore, cautionary tales passed on from generation to generation. These include scary creatures, mysterious places, confounding events and unresolved matters. Many believe these stories are based on truth; I do my best to explore that.

Legends and lore serve many purposes. For believers, these tales may simply document paranormal activity. For others, they may help explain that which is not easily explained. For others still, much like the experience of telling monster stories around a fire, such tales can be a fun escape from reality. Whatever the reason, these tales are a fascinating part of an area's history and reflect anxieties and fears in the country. There are intersections between cryptids, curses, lore, other supernatural storytelling and mysterious events with history, society, customs, cultural touchstones, politics and metaphors. Moreover, these stories are often at least based on underlying facts. Sometimes those facts have been spun into lore with the passage of time, and the tales evolve with each retelling. Maybe the stories are simply true from the start—you be the judge.

In my research, I have found there to be connections between folklore about cryptids, curses and other paranormal topics with underlying historical, societal and political facts. One example is the Salem witch trials of 1692 and 1693 in Massachusetts. The history is clear: nineteen people were tried and found guilty of witchcraft—in service to the devil—and executed. The Puritans, who founded Salem, were firm believers in the supernatural. The societal and political connections include a gender bias against women who made up most of the accused—a desire to "keep women in their place"—racial discrimination and economic battles between the haves and have-nots. Women had no legal identity as individuals. There was a belief that women had more difficulty than men in controlling irrational impulses and exhibiting extreme behavior. Women tended to resent this repression and treatment, and there was tension. Legal records were kept by men, legal proceedings were led by men and judges and juries were made up of men. The result was that women outnumbered men in being accused. More than two hundred were accused, and executed by hanging, with one

Salem Witch Trials, 2024. *Courtesy of Jason McLean*.

man pressed to death with stones. Thirteen of twenty women were hanged, with three additional women dying in prison. Society was led by repressive authority supported by religious anxiety. Additional historical elements included race and color—Tituba, one of the first to be accused, was an enslaved South American Indigenous Indian with dark skin. Further, there was friction between the rich and the poor, those with money and land, in this case primarily the merchant Porter family, and those without, mainly the farming Putnams, and their battle for power—and the young, the accusers, and old, the accused. These age-old societal battles were fought using the devil and witchcraft as proxies for the more real-world problems at play. Finally, the supernatural and paranormal beliefs were that the devil was possessing "afflicted" girl victims. Since the trials and executions, there have been many reports of spirits of those executed. Some of the reportedly most haunted locations are the Joshua Ward House (once owned by malicious sheriff George Corwin, who tortured victims and was cursed by eighty-one-year-old Giles Corey, who was pressed to death), the Witch House (once owned by Judge Jonathan Corwin, who sentenced victims to death) and the Old Burying Point Cemetery.

In my experience, some history purists bristle at the retelling of folkloric tales. They dispute the topics and events as "not history" and therefore of little or no value. I disagree. Although folklore is not regarded as history by some, to many—including the academic community—folklore is seen as an integral part of a region's history. Folklore is studied at Harvard, the University of California at Berkeley and other leading universities and is considered an important way to understand different cultures. Further, folklore—especially about the supernatural—draws the interest of people in a way that straight history too often does not. In this book, I intertwine folklore with history, and though I try to be clear about which is which, I believe the two go hand in hand.

I distinguish folklore from customs, as customs relate to behaviors and practices, not knowledge or belief, though they overlap in that people generally behave in a way that is in line with their society's beliefs.

America has several customs or practices many in the rest of the world find strange—many are quirky and funny. These include:

Presidential turkey pardons ahead of Thanksgiving
Holidays such as Groundhog Day in Pennsylvania, where a groundhog predicts the weather
Cherry pit spitting in Michigan

Turkey, 2024. *Courtesy of Jason McLean.*

Roadkill cook-offs in West Virginia

The National Hollerin' Contest in North Carolina

Pumpkin chucking in Delaware

Continued use of the imperial system of measurement—inches, feet, pounds, gallons, etc.—whereas much of the rest of the world uses the metric system

Using a primarily single-colored currency with similar-looking bills, whereas much of the rest of the world uses far more colorful money

Super-sizing fast food

Requesting condiments—ketchup, mustard, salt, etc.—with meals

Requesting "doggie" or to-go bags for unfinished restaurant food

Using a lot of ice in our drinks—in many other countries, that's looked at as "watering down" drinks

Giving a thumbs up—in fact, in some countries, it's seen as rude, like sticking up one's middle finger

A separate sales tax—in most other countries, this is already reflected in the item's price

Referring to the United States as "America"—it's considered politically incorrect in South America to refer to the United States in that way

Writing the date by month, day and year—most of the rest of the world uses day, month and year

Opening gifts in front of the gift giver—you may be seen as greedy for doing so

Requiring personal space with no physical contact

Tipping at restaurants

Chatting with strangers—in many other countries, people aren't as comfortable with this

Laughing out loud—in some Asian countries, it's considered rude to show your teeth

Expecting free refills of soft drinks and coffee

Going into debt for a college degree

Trick-or-treat practices—some countries don't see this as primarily for children

Sitting in the back seat of a taxi—in some other countries, that comes across as elitist

And staying optimistic, no matter the situation, is seen as a particularly American trait

Superstitions are like folklore in that they are often passed from one generation to the next and have their basis in stories dating back hundreds if not thousands of years. However, although there is overlap, unlike folkore, whose verity might be in question, superstition is more likely based on inaccurate assumptions, irrational fears, misunderstandings of science, obsessive-compulsive tendencies—uncontrollable, reoccurring thoughts, obsessions and behaviors—or other tricks of the mind. Superstitions can include fear of walking under ladders, stepping on a crack in the sidewalk or breaking a mirror, out of fear that something bad will come of it. Again, although many superstitions appear to be absurd on their face, sometimes they can become reality. "Never say never" is a good motto to use.

Urban legends, a type of contemporary folklore subcategory, are typically described as having happened to a family member or friend, not to the person telling the story—presumably to keep the teller of the story out of a negative light, with cautions about moral behavior. They tend to be relatively recent, not centuries old, and are often spread by word of mouth and newspapers, e-mail and social media. An example is the story of poisoned Halloween candy or candy with needles or razor blades placed in them by strangers to harm random children. These stories have been reported for about fifty years but appear to be generally false and alarmist, with there being very few people ever having been harmed in that way.

The definition of *legend* is a story from the past many people believe but that cannot be proven to be true. I would change the definition a little, ending with "has not yet been proven to be true." Again, keeping in mind what Thomas Edison said, I would never say never.

The following are many of the Pacific Northwest's dark folkloric tales.

Bandage Man

Humans have been frightened of boogeymen for as long as can be remembered. The Boogeyman comes in many iterations, with a general definition being a shadowy, amorphous (without a set appearance or structure) creature that hides in dark places, especially under beds, to frighten unsuspecting victims—many times children. Boogeymen are said to thrive on the fear of others, taking delight in their pain and suffering.

Bandage Man is a combination of the Boogeyman, a mummy and a zombie. Many parts of the country have somewhat similar creatures. Virginia has Bunny Man, dating to the 1970s, an escaped murderous convict who dressed in a bunny outfit at Halloween and committed paranormally related murders on Bunny Man Bridge. Hook Man is a Pennsylvania story that originated in the 1950s of a hook-handed lunatic who escaped from a mental institution and killed young couples parked at lovers' lanes. Lizard Man is a South Carolina legend about a slimy, seven-foot-tall green creature that attacked a man in 1988. Slender Man is an urban legend and viral internet creation that, it's said, drove two twelve-year-old girls in 2014 to stab a classmate nineteen times—she survived. Mothman is a West Virginia tale dating to 1966 when five men working at a cemetery saw a "brown being" emerge and fly away. Finally, the Jersey Devil dates to 1735 in New Jersey; it is said to be the thirteenth child—born with leathery wings, a goat's head, hooves, horns and a tail—killed its mother and family and caused panic. Local schools were closed in 1909 due to a supposed sighting. A modern animated version of the Boogeyman is the character Oogie Boogie in the 1993 movie *Nightmare Before Christmas*. He is a scary burlap sack filled with spiders and insects with a snake for his tongue. He is an evil and powerful creature and sings to Santa that he better listen to him because he's "the Boogeyman."

The Bandage Man legend dates to the late 1950s, with the story of a teenage couple who sat parked and making out in their pickup truck overlooking the Pacific Ocean near Cannon Beach, Oregon. Cannon Beach is a lovely little upscale oceanfront community named for a cannon that washed ashore from the sinking U.S. Navy schooner *Shark* in 1846. It was named by *National Geographic* in 2013 as one of the most beautiful places in the world. Suddenly, the couple felt the truck move violently as if someone had jumped into the cargo bed. They turned, looked through the back window and saw a disfigured man covered in bloody bandages, resembling a mummy, with his arms and legs protruding at odd angles as if he'd been in a terrible accident, rocking back and forth. He started beating on the back window and roof. They raced away, scared to death, down the highway, and when they looked back, the bandaged man had disappeared. It is thought Bandage Man is the tormented ghost of a disfigured logger killed in a horrific accident. The scent of rotting flesh and bloody bandages lingers even after Bandage Man vanishes. Others have since reported seeing Bandage Man jumping into open truck beds and convertible cars' backseats. Still others say they've seen him walking along the beach, down Highway 101 and on a short road called Bandage Man Road. There are also stories of Bandage Man smashing the windows of a local business and even eating someone's dog. Another legend reports that the Bandage Man story dates to the 1930s, when a logger was badly injured in logging activities. An ambulance came for the logger, who was wrapped in bandages. However, that ambulance was damaged by a landslide while en route to the hospital on old Highway 101. The injured logger was reportedly gone when the rescue crew arrived at the landslide location and searched for him.

Bandage Man was the subject of a 1974 University of Oregon Northwest folklore research study titled "The Bandage Man Legend: A Cannon Beach Legend." The study explores the horrific tales and legends that have been passed down since the 1950s. He was the focus of a 2003 horror-comedy film titled *Bandage Man*, directed by multiple-award-winning Irish filmmaker Ivan Kavanagh. The movie stays relatively true to the legend. It tells of a man who regularly travels on the Highway 26 overpass at night, despite warnings not to do so. As it turns out, the man is looking for Bandage Man, whom he visits weekly to provide him with another dog to eat. In 2020, after I had written several Halloween-related articles for the *Astorian* newspaper in Astoria, Oregon, including some about Bandage Man, a woman reached out to me through the editor. She swore Bandage Man had visited her in her bedroom in Cannon Beach one night and acted like he was going to attack her, only to disappear. She was very serious and said this was the first time she'd ever experienced anything like it.

As I've mentioned, I find a strong correlation between historical events and several purported paranormal activities—I mentioned the Salem Witch Trials and the treatment of women, the rich versus the poor, race and color, etc., in New England in the 1690s. First, related to Bandage Man, logging has been an important activity in the Pacific Northwest for well over one hundred years and is very dangerous, with horrible accidents happening. Second, in the 1950s in America, there was a strong stigma against premarital sex. In 1969, 70 percent of Americans disapproved of premarital sex, but by 1973, this number had dropped to 50 percent. It is thought, by those who don't believe in the folkloric tale, that the Bandage Man story—like some similar boogeyman stories—was based on the desire to scare teens and others into more chaste behavior. It always surprises me that, even though the Bandage Man story has existed for about seventy years, most people in the Pacific Northwest I've talked with have never heard of him.

Billy Gohl

Aberdeen, Washington, is and was a hardworking seafaring town, founded in 1884. By the late nineteenth century, the town had become a hotbed of many shady activities, including wild saloons, gambling and brothels, earning it the nickname the "Hellhole of the Pacific." Other nicknames were the "Port of Missing Men" and the "Floater Fleet," reflecting the disappearances, murder and bodies of sailors found floating in the nearby Wishkah River and others who were passing through.

Billy Gohl, nicknamed the "Ghoul of Grays Harbor" and the "Timber Town Killer," resided in Aberdeen in the late nineteenth and early twentieth centuries. Gohl may have been one of the worst—yet least remembered— serial killers, murdering his victims one at a time, in different places, versus mass murderers, who typically commit their murders at one time, in one place, in American history. Legend has it that although he was convicted of murdering two men, he may have murdered well over one hundred. It seems the worst monsters may in fact be human.

An imposing figure at six feet, two inches tall and powerfully built, the German-born Gohl had failed as a gold prospector in the Yukon. He worked for a time on San Francisco's wharves before becoming a bartender.

In 1903, Gohl moved to Aberdeen, where he worked as an official for the Sailor's Union of the Pacific (SUP). About a year after Gohl's arrival in Aberdeen, the number of "floaters"—lifeless bodies found floating in the water—dramatically increased around the Wishkah River and Grays Harbor. The SUP building served as the center for Gohl's unsavory activities. Sailors, new to the area, would inevitably visit the union hall in search of a job or, if they were already a member, to take care of personal business. Gohl would inquire whether the sailors had family or friends in the area. The topic would then shift to that of money and belongings. If the sailor had items to steal and he wouldn't be missed by family or friends, Gohl would make the unfortunate his next murder victim. Gohl's preferred method of murder was shooting, but poisoning, strangling and bludgeoning were also employed. He would dispose of the corpses in the Wishkah River, which ran behind the union hall and into Grays Harbor. Some say Gohl used a trapdoor and chute in his office to carry his victims to the river.

Gohl was arrested in February 1910 and admitted his guilt for two murders. He claimed there was no trapdoor and said that if there had been one, it would open only into the saloon, not the river. Gohl recounted what he would do if a sailor came into the SUP office and gave Gohl personal belongings, including money, to store for him. Gohl would tell the sailor that a "scab" boat was coming in and that the sailor should dress in a logger's outfit to wait on a piling at the dock for the boat. Gohl would then get his rifle, aim through his office's window and shoot the sailor in the head.

Gohl was found guilty of the two murders on May 12, 1910, and sentenced to two consecutive life terms at Washington's Walla Walla state penitentiary. Gohl was later moved to the Eastern State Psychiatric Hospital—established in 1891 and still in operation—in Spokane County, Washington. It was said Gohl went insane due to either a stabbing he witnessed in prison or complications from syphilis. He died in the asylum in 1927. Gohl is buried in Eastern State Psychiatric Hospital's Cemetery No. 1 in an unmarked grave. There are at least 4,440 unmarked and mixed gravesites there, and some of the remains have been reburied several times. With Gohl's resting place there, it is said to be cursed and not the best place to visit at night, as sightings of his ghost have been reported.

In modern-day Aberdeen, Billy's Bar & Grill (the same building from which Gohl committed his murders; I can attest they have excellent cheeseburgers!), named after the serial killer, Gohl's ghost and the spirits of

PACIFIC NORTHWEST LEGENDS AND LORE

his victims have been seen. The sights and sounds of lights turning on and off, disembodied voices and sailors in early twentieth-century clothing, as well as the feeling of cold spots, are commonplace. Drinking glasses have been seen flying before smashing against the wall.

Black-Eyed Children

Black-Eyed Children may be one of the weirder—and that's saying something—aspects of Pacific Northwest folklore, although they occur elsewhere as well. They seem to be primarily an Internet-fueled urban legend of paranormal creatures, said to resemble children, usually aged six to sixteen. They are described as having pale skin and blacked-out eyes—devoid of sclera or iris. Most often they are encountered on dark, empty roads late at night, hitchhiking, begging, approaching stopped cars and residences—asking if they can use your telephone to call their parents. Sometimes their attire appears outdated, and some have been described as having talon-like feet. These legendary beings approach their victim asking for simple favors—food, money, shelter, to use the phone, etc.—and then their victim is suddenly overwhelmed with a feeling of being sick with dread and despair. Black-Eyed Children don't seem to do anything to cause this feeling but are described as "chilling," said to give off "wretched vibes" and feelings of dread before leaving.

Some stories say the children are aliens, while others describe them as demons. Pets, especially cats, seem to recognize these beings as something other than humans, reacting with fright and anger. Some pets are said to die soon after the encounter. Other stories say the beings can cause those encountering them to suffer nosebleeds and electrical disturbances—lights going out, etc. Black-eyed children stories seem to have started in the 1980s, including one being seen in Portland, Oregon. They have been featured in the 2012 movie titled *Black Eyed Kids*, in a 2013 episode of Microsoft Network's (MSN) *Weekly Strange* and on the television program *Monsters and Mysteries in America*.

Cat Serial Killer

I mentioned earlier in the cat-like cryptids section that cats, throughout history, have alternatively been viewed as good-luck charms, deities and harbingers of evil. Some attribute supernatural powers to cats. Many of these stories appear to be based on an underlying fear of cats. Someone took this apparent hate of cats to a new extreme in a disturbing real-world story in 2018. Someone—we may never know who—killed thirteen cats in the city of Olympia, Washington. But they didn't just kill the cats; he or she surgically mutilated them—some reports say their spines were removed. The mutilations were done with almost expert-level skills, by someone seemingly with medical expertise, like what serial killer Jack the Ripper was said to have done in England in the late nineteenth century to his female victims. The killer then ritualistically displayed and "splayed" the dead and mutilated cats in public places throughout the city. The newspapers described these events as "disturbing and scary." I've spoken with cat owners and other residents who said they were scared to death as these events unfolded. The authorities took these events seriously, formed a ten-person task force, and offered a $53,000 reward. On one of my history and haunted tours of Olympia, a former police officer who was on the task force confirmed the facts I just mentioned. The cat serial killer has never been found. People in Olympia hope the killer never again strikes to terrorize the city and cat owners in particular.

Chinatowns

Throughout much of the nineteenth century, many in the Pacific Northwest White community viewed Natives as their primary adversaries. By the 1880s, after Natives had been mostly neutralized by war and treaties and relegated to reservations, some White settlers began to view Chinese residents as the enemy—I mentioned this earlier in discussing the Bellingham curse. Chinese immigrants came to the Pacific Northwest in the early 1870s to build railroads and work in mining, salmon canning and agriculture. Many of the unemployed White residents viewed the Chinese as unfair competition for the jobs that existed. Under the nationwide 1882 Chinese Exclusion Act, the Chinese were ineligible for U.S. citizenship and not able to apply for homesteads or to own land. These events took a darker turn when, in September 1885, miners in Wyoming attacked Chinese miners, driving them from town and killing many. This act emboldened radical anti-Chinese sentiment in the Pacific Northwest and elsewhere.

On September 5, 1885, in present-day Issaquah, Washington, east of Seattle, three Chinese workers were shot to death in their sleep by alleged White killers, who were exonerated. On November 3, 1885, a Tacoma,

Chinatown, San Francisco, 2012. *Courtesy of Library of Congress, Carol M. Highsmith, photographer.*

Washington mob led by Mayor Weisbach marched on the Chinese community, forced residents out of and burned their houses and businesses and shipped them to Portland, Oregon. Weisbach had held mass meetings to plan on ousting the Chinese and distributed flyers that read "The Chinese Must Go!" Some Seattle citizens tried to do the same, but Washington territorial governor Watson Squire called in federal troops and declared martial law, stopping the mob. Vigilantes in the town of Tenino, Washington, burned Chinese residents out of their homes on Christmas Eve 1885. On February 7, 1886, Seattle mobs were successful in herding the city's 350 Chinese residents on to a steamship, which took them out of the city to Port Townsend to the north, Tacoma to the south and elsewhere in the Pacific Northwest. On February 8, 1886, in Olympia, the mob's prearranged signal of ringing the city fire bell took place. Agitators attempted to expel Chinese residents, converging on their dwellings. However, Sheriff William Billings deputized prominent Olympia residents to patrol the area, and they stopped the mob from achieving their goal. No Chinese were forced to leave their homes in Olympia, although discrimination continued. Two Portland Chinatown buildings were burned down in the mid-1880s, accompanied by anti-Chinese rallies. In 1887, thirty-four Chinese gold miners in Oregon's

Wallowa County's Hells Canyon, on the border with Idaho, were robbed, murdered and mutilated by horse thieves who were White. No one was ever punished, and the name of one of the murderers' leaders, "Old Blue" Bruce Evans, was engraved on the Wallowa, Oregon courthouse arch as one of the area's first settlers. In 2005, the United States renamed the area in which the murders took place, along the Snake River, as "Chinese Massacre Cove."

This dark chapter in the Pacific Northwest's history—the mobs' despicable behavior, the bravery of other citizens and the Chinese communities' courage—make this a sad story but one of resilience. Today, Chinese Americans are an important part of the diverse community of the Pacific Northwest.

Columbia River Gorge

Oregon's Columbia River Gorge is an amazing river canyon, four thousand feet deep and eighty miles long—some call it the "Grand Canyon of the Pacific Northwest." The Gorge is a place of special significance to Natives, who believe spirits formed the area. One of their best-known stories is about the Bridge of the Gods, in which two brothers fought over a woman named Loowit and caused an ancient bridge to collapse into the Gorge. A modern cantilever toll bridge by the same name now spans the Columbia River in the same spot at Cascade Locks in Oregon. The Gorge is a major tourist area, both for its natural beauty and its paranormal tales.

Despite its idyllic setting, the Gorge has seemingly more than its fair share of strange, possibly paranormal occurrences and lore. I mentioned earlier,

Columbia River Gorge, 1936.
Courtesy of Library of Congress, Arthur Rothstein.

there are reports of Bigfoot, the Klickitat Ape Cat, sea serpents and other cryptids in and around the Gorge. The Gorge also has several reportedly paranormally laden hotels. McMenamins', known as the supernatural hotel and restaurant chain, has forty-six businesses in Oregon and ten in Washington, and the business seems to embrace its reputation. Edgefield Hotel in Troutdale was formerly the old Multnomah County Poor Farm, where care was given to those who either couldn't or wouldn't care for themselves, built in 1911. It is regularly listed as one of the most haunted hotels in America. Guests have reported a ghostly woman reciting nursery rhymes and a woman in white wandering the grounds. On one of my history and haunted walking tours of Olympia, a woman described visiting the Edgefield and having an unseen force tug on her jacket. She took it to mean that a spirit was letting her know that it was present. The Hood River Hotel was established in 1912 and is said to be haunted by original owner Ola Bell. Visitors report disembodied footsteps, doorknobs turning on their own and phantom phone calls. The Columbia Gorge Hotel, constructed in 1921, has experienced mysterious fires, furniture and other objects moving on their own and vacant rooms being barricaded from the inside.

D.B. Cooper

American folklore is full of stories about D.B. Cooper, who committed the United States' only unsolved aircraft hijacking over the Columbia River, separating Oregon and Washington. To this day, we do not know who Cooper is or was, where he came from or where he went—it is one of America's greatest mysteries. There have been many television programs and movies featuring the story of D.B. Cooper, including one of my favorite adventure comedies—2004's *Without a Paddle*.

The day before Thanksgiving, November 24, 1971, a man in his mid-forties wearing dark sunglasses boarded a Northwest Orient, now part of Delta Airlines, airliner at Portland International Airport. His ticket was for Dan Cooper, he sat in seat 18F and he almost immediately ordered water with bourbon. Later, a law enforcement official erroneously referred to Cooper as "D.B." and the abbreviation stuck. Once the Boeing 727 was airborne, Cooper handed a flight attendant a note reading: "Miss, I've got a bomb, come sit next to me you're being hijacked." Cooper opened his briefcase, which looked to contain an explosive, and then demanded $200,000 in cash and two parachutes. His demands were met on landing

Jetliner, 2024. *Courtesy of Jason McLean.*

at Seattle-Tacoma International Airport, where he released passengers and two flight attendants. Cooper then directed the pilot to take off again and fly at an altitude of ten thousand feet—low enough for someone to parachute from the airplane—as the airliner made its way to Mexico City, by way of Reno, Nevada. Forty minutes into this portion of the flight, a signal in the cockpit showed the plane's rear stairway had been lowered. The stairs were down, and two parachutes, the money and Cooper were all missing when the jet touched down in Reno. It is presumed Cooper parachuted out of the plane somewhere over the Oregon-Washington border, near Portland and the Columbia River. A bundle of $20 bills was discovered by a child in 1980 when he was digging in a sand bar along the north bank of the Columbia River, west of Vancouver, Washington. The bills' serial numbers matched some of the ransom money. Law enforcement has Cooper's fingerprints from an in-flight magazine and DNA from the black tie Cooper was wearing before he jumped.

There have been numerous deathbed confessions and other claims of Cooper's discovery and/or copycat confessions of guilt. These include John List, a fugitive accused of murdering his family in New Jersey days before the hijacking; a man named Duane Weber who had been in prison near Seattle and told his wife in a 1995 deathbed confession that he was Cooper; and Kenneth Christiansen, a former paratrooper and employee of Northwest Orient airline. The FBI continues to follow up on leads in the case, with no clear end in sight. Law enforcement is literally chasing the "ghost" of D.B. Cooper, and it is difficult to predict the outcome of the search for the man some view as a modern-day Robin Hood.

New evidence found by an investigator and reported in January 2024 indicates, based on state-of-the-art analysis, three stainless steel and titanium fragments found on D.B. Cooper's tie may be traced to a specific Pennsylvania steel company. That company, Crucible Steel, worked closely with Boeing on aircraft manufacturing. The investigator stated his belief that the findings point to Crucible's titanium research engineer at the time—I'm leaving his name out of this writing. If true, that person—now dead—would have had in-depth and extensive knowledge of the Boeing 727 jetliner involved in the hijacking. The alleged hijacker also would have been familiar with Seattle, where Boeing manufacturing took place and the aircraft was forced to land during the hijacking. Finally, Crucible suffered a significant downtown in 1971, and that could have served as motivation, if Cooper was an employee, for the hijacking.

Dead Zone

Many American cities, including Portland, Oregon and Seattle, have a history of red-light districts, often called "tenderloins," where prostitution and other illegal activities took place. These red-light districts were parts of the cities devoted to vice, criminal and unsavory activity such as prostitution, gambling, opium dens, shanghaiing—discussed later—and more. The name *tenderloin* came from a New York City police captain who gave the area its

Olympia, Washington, 1901. *Courtesy of Library of Congress, U.S. Geog. File.*

nickname in 1876, remarking that he could afford tenderloin steak from the bribes he was receiving.

A typical red-light district existed in Olympia, Washington, from 1880 until the 1910s. This tenderloin district was officially called the "Dead Zone" by the Olympia City Council. The history of this district officially started with the 1860 Olympia Ordinance 145, which was enacted to prohibit nuisances such as prostitution, "squaw" dancing—paying a woman to dance; I had to research what it meant—brothels, gambling, drunkenness, opium and other vices. By 1880, it was clear the ordinance had little or no effect, and the Olympia City Council declared the area north of State Avenue as a "dead zone," where the ordinance would not be enforced. Rather, the police chief collected monthly fees from Dead Zone business owners and residents. In December 1892, in a widely reported incident, one prostitute took the name "Dead Zone" to heart. Juanita Ursula "Gypsy Ashton" Unfug married and murdered Thomas Henderson Boyd, owner and editor of the *Morning Olympian* newspaper. Another feature of the Dead Zone was the large number of illegitimate children born to sex workers. These babies, who were left on residents' doorsteps to hopefully be adopted, were referred to as "doorstep babies." The best known of these children grew up to be Jesse Truman Trullinger, Washington State attorney general and Olympia mayor from 1941 to 1946.

The story of Emma Merlotin, whose real name was Anne Jeanne Tingry-LeCoz, is perhaps Portland, Oregon's best-known paranormal story. Born in France in 1850, Merlotin was a prostitute working in Portland's Tenderloin District, also known as the "Court of Death"—due to the great number of prostitutes murdered there in the 1880s. The authorities seemingly did little to stop the slayings, possibly due to a bias against prostitutes. On December 22, 1885, a cold and rainy night, the thirty-five-year-old Merlotin was brutally hacked to death with a hatchet. A police officer heard her screams and found her just before 11:00 p.m., lying face down in a three-foot-wide puddle of blood. She suffered gruesome bludgeoning and slashing, with twelve wounds to her head and arms. Portland police first thought the motive was robbery, but they soon found a gold ring that had fallen off her finger on the floor nearby. She was also still wearing her gold earrings and had $15 on her person—about $500 today. A sailor, William Sundstrom, was arrested "prowling around" the murder scene and trying to enter Merlotin's cottage. He had a badly scratched face, which he claimed was due to his "falling against a tree trunk," bloody pants and a bloody hatchet at his house. Though he claimed the hatchet was covered in red paint, it was found to be blood. While police arrested Sundstrom, they did not charge him or anyone else with Merlotin's murder. There is no apparent reason for this other than, perhaps, a bias against prostitutes. Merlotin was buried in Portland's Lone Fir Cemetery—established 1855—where visitors have reported seeing a shadowy female figure dressed in nineteenth-century French fashion roaming the cemetery. When approached, the figure throws up her hands, screams and vanishes.

Because 1880s scientists believed, since debunked, the last thing a person saw before death was preserved in their retinas—termed retinal optography—one of Merlotin's eyes was removed and given to a well-known local photographer for later study; it was lost to history.

First Flying Saucer

We tend to think of unidentified flying objects (UFOs) as a modern phenomenon. Numerous books, television programs and movies have been made about them, including two Steven Spielberg movies about friendly aliens: 1977's *Close Encounters of the Third Kind* and 1982's *E.T. the Extra-Terrestrial*; less-than-friendly aliens, including 1979's *Alien* and 1953's and

Flying saucer, 2024. *Courtesy of Jason McLean.*

2005's *The War of the Worlds* (based on the 1898 H.G. Wells novel); and many others. In fact, the first reported UFO sighting in America was by the Puritans in 1639. John Winthrop, governor of the Massachusetts Bay Colony, observed and wrote about a mysterious bright light in the evening sky. He described it as about three yards square and as swift as an arrow, darting back and forth. Winthrop made it clear it was strange and wasn't something he'd seen before.

Since the 1940s and 1950s, there have been numerous UFO sightings. These sightings may have been influenced by the tension caused by the Cold War between the United States and the Soviet Union. There's also little doubt that our own space exploration programs, including landing on the moon, have fed these interests since. They may also be real.

The first time the term *flying saucer* was used related to an incident in the Pacific Northwest. On June 24, 1947, pilot Kenneth A. Arnold—he was also a politician, winning the Republican nomination for Idaho lieutenant governor in 1962—was flying his small private plane by Washington's Mount Rainier. He was on his way from Chehalis, Washington, to an air show in Pendleton, Oregon. He was an experienced pilot, having flown four thousand hours, and was a member of Idaho Search and Rescue. Arnold was keeping his eyes out for the wreckage of a U.S. Marine transport aircraft that had crashed along his route, with thirty-two servicemen dying. Twenty miles west of the mountain, he saw what he assumed was the bright reflection off a U.S. military airplane. Instead, what he saw were nine large shiny circular objects, flying in a *V* formation, each 100 feet across—the size of one-third of a football field or the length of a blue whale. Arnold said they resembled saucers if you skipped them across water. The objects flipped, banked and weaved back and forth in controlled flight. Arnold estimated the objects were flying between 1,200 and 1,700 miles per hour. The *East Oregonian* newspaper, mistaking Arnold as saying the vehicles were shaped like saucers, versus moving like them, printed an article the day after the sighting describing the objects as "saucer-like." The *Chicago Sun* ran a story titled "Supersonic Flying Saucers Sighted by Idaho Pilot." A prospector on Washington's nearby Mount Adams also saw the flying objects, corroborating Arnold's story. Later, in July 1947, a Roswell, New Mexico newspaper claimed the U.S. Army had recovered a flying saucer by the nearby base. The army said it was a wrecked weather balloon. The U.S. Air Force investigated and, in a 1948 operation called "Sign," found Arnold and the prospector to be credible witnesses but determined they had seen a mirage. They, as well as subsequent government investigations, have found no credibility to the Roswell story.

Arnold's story may have involved the first use of *flying saucer*, as subsequent sightings used that phrase. He maintained his story was accurate until his death in 1984.

Forest Man

Forest Man, or just Man, is a creature that lives in heavily wooded areas of the Pacific Northwest's Puget Sound—from Olympia, Washington, in the south to the Strait of Juan de Fuca, separating Washington from British Columbia, Canada, in the north. Many liken the Man to shadow people—a shadow in humanoid form, thought to be a ghost or other supernatural entity. It is said the Man can take human form and will often approach rural homes during the day asking for money or a ride to Seattle. If they decline the requests, the Forest Man will become hostile but won't enter the home until nightfall, when he will terrorize the homeowner. If the homeowner gives the Man money, he will return to the forest. If they give him a ride to Seattle, they will never reencounter the Forest Man, but their car will always smell like sulfur. If you are hiking through the forest and suddenly feel like you're being watched, that may be the Forest Man.

Fort Stevens

As of this writing, Fort Stevens in Warrenton, Oregon, is the only U.S. military base in the contiguous United States (lower forty-eight states) attacked by a foreign power since the War of 1812. In 1942, a Japanese submarine lobbed bombs into the fort, no one was killed. Touring, as I have done, the fort's abandoned historic structures can be unnerving. Guests and state park staff have described seeing the phantoms of soldiers—one in full battle gear, one carrying a long knife and another carrying a lantern— wandering the fort's grounds, appearing to be in search of possible enemy soldiers. Two of the ghostly soldiers appear to be dressed in Civil War–era uniforms—the fort was from the Civil War era, built in 1863—while the other was dressed in World War II–era clothes. A man described walking

Fort Stevens, Oregon, 2018. *Courtesy of Library of Congress, Carol M. Highsmith, photographer.*

around the grounds and seeing a soldier dressed in a World War II uniform. The man and the ghostly soldier nodded to each other as they passed, but when the man turned around, the soldier was gone. In another story, visitors to the fort were chased by a World War II–clothed full-body apparition threatening them with a knife. Although no lives were lost in the Japanese attack, it appears the resulting trauma has somehow scarred the base-leaving paranormal entities and supernatural events. Ghost stories, although often based where lives were lost, can also take place where traumatic and other high-energy events occurred.

Grandpa

Owners of Seattle-area homes built after the Great Seattle Fire of 1889 may find a unique individual living in their crawlspace or dusty attic, known as "Grandpa." The old downtown, now the Pioneer Square area, was mostly destroyed, with few deaths during the fire, but many lives were lost during the cleanup. This paranormal character, with seemingly supernatural abilities, is known only through its actions—perhaps a broken teacup or a window left open. If this haunting happens to you, Grandpa can be appeased by the afflicted party leaving nickels, face up, on the threshold of every in-house bathroom. Remember to replenish any nickels that go missing. Grandpa is said to be mainly benevolent and will ensure your early spring flowers won't freeze or grow before their time. This legend may be in response to the catastrophic impacts of the Great Fire and the emotional toll it took on Seattle's residents.

Graveyard of the Pacific

I describe the Graveyard of the Pacific earlier, in the introductory section. The more than 2,000 ships and countless lives lost—primarily in the late nineteenth and early twentieth centuries, but shipwrecks continue—are overwhelmingly higher than those of the legendary and some say paranormal waters of the Bermuda Triangle, which experienced 50 ships and 20 airplanes lost. One of the best places to learn more about the Graveyard is at the Columbia River Maritime Museum in Astoria, Oregon, where, in 2021, I spoke and "launched" my first book *Haunted Graveyard of the Pacific*. Interestingly, North Carolina's Outer Banks has a similar area called the

Shipwrecked, late nineteenth century. *Courtesy of Library of Congress.*

"Graveyard of the Atlantic," with more than 5,000 shipwrecks and countless lives lost dating back to the 1500s. The greatest number of shipwrecks in the United States occurred in the Great Lakes, in the central-eastern part of the country, with some 6,000 ships lost, 1,500 of them in Michigan waters. One of these ships was the *Edmund Fitzgerald,* which sank in 1975 in Lake Superior and is immortalized in the 1976 Gordon Lightfoot song "The Wreck of the Edmund Fitzgerald."

Supernatural lore abounds in the Graveyard of the Pacific, no doubt related to the calamities having taken place there. The combination of river flow and offshore currents creates an ever-shifting hazardous sand bar at the mouth of the 1,214-mile-long Columbia River—one of the longest rivers in the United States—and unlike other rivers, whose power dissipates as it drains into deltas, the Columbia River funnels water like a powerful fire hose into the Pacific Ocean. This, together with the presence of thick fog, violent storms and concealed sand bars prior to the time of GPS, satellites and other technology caused ships to sink, burn and be crushed against the shore. Mariners and passengers have been swallowed by the waters for as long as can be remembered. The Graveyard has a reportedly high level of paranormal activity. On land, sailors were shanghaied or kidnapped for involuntary service onboard ships, women were kidnapped for prostitution and slavery and lighthouse keepers and their families suffered tragic deaths— as mentioned in the earlier discussion on Cape Disappointment. Other lingering spirits are said to include those of early settlers, Natives whose lands were stolen and burial grounds desecrated, murderers and murder victims and soldiers.

Shipwreck, 2024. *Courtesy of Jason McLean.*

The worst shipwreck in the Graveyard of the Pacific was the overloaded—gold miners and others were thought to have climbed aboard just before sailing—and beyond its prime sidewheeler *Pacific*, which was built in 1850 and left Victoria, British Columbia, on November 4, 1875, on its way to San Francisco and collided with the sailing ship *Orpheus* off the Washington coast. While *Orpheus* was left relatively unscathed, the *Pacific* disintegrated into the ocean with its estimated over five hundred passengers and crew spilling into the Pacific. There were only three survivors. The *Pacific* had previously been mothballed in Sacramento but was put back into service due to the gold rush that was taking place (the San Francisco 49ers football team was named for the prospectors of the earlier California gold rush). Workers in Sacramento reported the *Pacific*'s wood was so rotten, they could scrape it out with their fingernails. Also, they observed rats running off the ship, a bad sign; see the section on nautical superstitions.

An additional Graveyard of the Pacific shipwreck involved the sidewheeler *General Warren*, which struck land in heavy weather on January 31, 1852, with forty-two men and women on board. When the *General Warren* began leaking, Captain Charles Thompson launched a small boat with ten men on board to seek help in nearby Astoria, Oregon. On reaching Astoria, the crew sought and received help, and when the combined crew and rescuers returned to the scene of the disaster, to their horror, they found no remnants of the wreck, passengers or crew. Thirty-two had perished, the only survivors being the ten who sought help. Two victims' bodies washed ashore a few days later: a newlywed couple on their way to San Francisco for their honeymoon. It was reported by the local newspaper that the groom had $160 in his jacket pocket, and the bride had a gold ring, engraved with a heart, on her left ring finger. They were said to be holding hands—possibly the newspaper sensationalizing the story—when they were found washed ashore. There are stories of paranormal cries and moans carried on the wind attributed to the newlyweds' ghosts.

Green River Killer

Gary Leon Ridgway was one of the worst serial killers in American history. His story has been featured in several television programs, movies and other popular media, including the 2005 movie *Green River Killer*. He was arrested in November 2001 and convicted of forty-nine murders of women committed between the early 1980s and late 1990s. He confessed to killing up to eighty. Many of his victims were prostitutes and runaways from in and around King County in Washington. He received his nickname based on his first five victims, who were found around the Green River, that starts in the Cascade Mountains east of Seattle. Ridgway terrorized the Pacific Northwest with his murderous activity and ability to evade authorities searching for him. Some strange facts about this case include Ridgway being able to pass a lie detector test in 1984 despite his answering "No" to the question of whether he had ever caused the death of a prostitute. The police sought and received serial killer Ted Bundy's—discussed elsewhere—help in identifying the murderer. Bundy correctly observed the murderer was mild-mannered and seemingly inoffensive. Ridgway confessed to having sex with his dead victims and having to bury them in order stop from going back to them. Ridgway was a Vietnam War veteran who was married twice unsuccessfully—he married a third time before becoming highly religious. His father had voiced criticism of prostitutes in and around Sea-Tac Airport south of Seattle, and he became a critic too. This didn't stop him from being a client of the sex workers before murdering them. Ridgway was identified based on DNA evidence. At this writing, Ridgway is seventy-four years old and serving a life sentence in Washington's Walla Walla state penitentiary. On one of my history and haunted walking tours of Olympia, a woman mentioned hearing of a modern-day Satanic ritual, including beheading chickens, at the Green River—apparently seeking to use the negative paranormal energy left by the killings to summon evil spirits. Ick!

Mosquito Fleet

From the 1880s to the 1920s, the primary way in which people traveled in the Puget Sound region, from Olympia, Washington, in the south to the Strait of Juan de Fuca in the north, was on the hundreds of small steamboats that plied the waters. They were known as the Mosquito Fleet. The forest was too dense to ride horses and maneuver wagons, and roads wouldn't be built until the 1930s. Two million people a year traveled aboard the small wooden steamboats. The boats stopped at virtually every waterfront dock, were often jerry rigged and sometimes less than seaworthy. Further, their captains and crews differed in levels of competence. Collisions and other accidents were not uncommon at a time before depth-sonar and GPS. This led to at least seventy-three shipwrecks.

The worst shipwreck on Puget Sound involved the *Dix*, a 102-foot, 130-ton vessel, that wrecked on November 18, 1906. That day, the ship steamed from the Seattle dock to Bainbridge Island with seventy-seven on board. The *Dix* was piloted by a confused and unlicensed ship's first officer by the name of Charles Dennison. Captain Percy Lermond, as many captains did, was collecting fares. There was no lookout watching for obstacles, and two miles west of Alki, the first officer steered the Mosquito Fleet steamer into the much larger four-masted steam schooner *Jeanie*—186 feet long, 1,000

Steamboat, 1890.
Courtesy of Library of Congress.

tons. The *Dix* rolled like a log, split in two and sank within five minutes, killing forty-five of the seventy-seven on board. It was a starry night and the ship's speed was slow, but the *Dix* was top-heavy. The ship's wreck remains six hundred feet underwater in Puget Sound; victims' bodies were never recovered, nor were pieces of the vessel. I refer to Puget Sound as a "watery graveyard" given the ships and crews that lie at its bottom.

While the *Dix* was Puget Sound's worst maritime disaster, it was Washington's second-worst transportation disaster, behind the 1910 Wellington train wrecks at Stevens Pass, Washington, caused by an avalanche, that killed ninety-six passengers on two trains. The *Dix*'s captain survived, but his license was revoked. It was later reinstated, but only to captain cargo ships. I discuss another famous Puget Sound shipwreck, the *Andelana*, in the section on curses.

Old Hotel Olympian

The Old Hotel Olympian in Olympia, Washington, was built in 1919 and has served as a senior residence center since 1975. There are stories of a Prohibition-era (1920–33) tunnel, when the sale and consumption of alcohol were banned, under the building to transport alcohol to the Old State Capitol across the street for state legislators to drink; that building served as Washington's capitol from 1905 to 1928. There are also urban legends of an "underground city" under the hotel, with old shops, storefronts, sidewalks and brothels—like but much smaller than Seattle's underground, discussed later. The underground is said to lie behind a heavily chained and locked door. Finally, there are ghost stories related to the Urban Onion Restaurant that was in the building for decades, it closed in 2015. One account describes how all chairs were pushed under dining tables upon closing the restaurant for the night. The next morning, employees found the chairs pushed away from the tables by some unseen force. Employees said, "No one wants to work here alone at night."

Olympia Saved by Beer

On May 18, 1882, the city of Olympia, Washington, experienced a major fire that threatened the entire downtown. As mentioned regarding Portland, Oregon and Seattle, many towns and cities in the Pacific Northwest and elsewhere, suffered from fires in the late nineteenth century. Olympia had three in 1882 and 1883, and Tacoma, Washington, had three in 1884. This again was because cities were built almost entirely of wood, and fire departments were not effective. In May 1882, Olympia experienced dry weather and suffered from weak pressure supplying water to the city's fire hydrants. The fire started at the Vienna Restaurant and spread to a grocery store, Doane's Oyster House next door, the post office, a dry goods store and Talcott's jewelry store. It had burned down an entire city block by the time it threatened the Lost Beer Hall. Beer Hall owner Phillip Hiltz saw an opportunity amid the flames and ash. While the fire raged, Hiltz offered cash to the owner of the next-door *Olympia Courier Newspaper* to buy that building. The building owner agreed and handed over the deed in exchange for cash. Hiltz then went to the firefighters and offered them a full day of free, unlimited beer and other alcohol if they would put out the fire and save the remaining buildings—including Hiltz's recent acquisition. The firefighters were able to put out the fire and received their reward of free alcohol for a day. The city went on to replace wooden structures with those made of stone and brick, reorganized the fire department and bought new firefighting equipment. When I tell this story on the history and haunted folklore tours I lead of Olympia's downtown historic district, locals and visitors alike are surprised and amused by these historic events.

Oregon Trail

The nineteenth-century Oregon Trail stretched approximately two thousand miles west from Missouri toward the Rocky Mountains and ended in Oregon's Willamette Valley. It was a major land route for those wishing to travel west, with 300,000 to 400,000 immigrants traveling the route between 1840 and 1860. Awaiting these travelers was inexpensive, fertile land. Pioneers had to use ingenuity, such as using wild animal feces instead of wood to build fires. The dangers and opportunities represented by the Trail have served as subjects for many books, television programs and movies, including 1959's *The Oregon Trail*.

The trail was dangerous; over thirty thousand lives were lost, one in ten migrants. Tremendous hardship and death were a too frequent occurrence for travelers along the trail. It is estimated that ten graves were dug every mile to bury the dead. Most deaths occurred due to diseases caused by poor sanitation, such as cholera, dysentery, scurvy and typhoid fever, as well as measles, smallpox and others. Another major cause of death for adults and children was falling off wagons and getting run over. Many pioneers purchased firearms for protection—there was no law enforcement present—the first weapons they had owned, and mishaps occurred, causing injury and death. Other deaths on the trail were due to drowning in rivers, suicide, weather, stampeding livestock, wild animals, fellow migrant attacks, lightning, tornados and gunpowder explosions. There were few doctors, but with medical science in its infancy, they often caused bad to get worse, such as bleeding for fever, using mercury or opium in medicines and so on. Migrants became accustomed to death, suffering each loss together, quickly burying their dead and pressing on in hopes of a better life.

There were some conflicts between Natives and migrants along the trail, but they were relatively rare. It is estimated that between 1840 and 1860, Natives killed 362 migrants, and migrants killed 426 Natives. Bad advice and directions made things worse, such as the Hastings Cutoff, which put pioneers in harm's way, with boulders, deep water, dead-end canyons and worse. The most horrible story of the Oregon Trail was the Donner Party, 1846–47, which turned to cannibalism; 45 of 81 travelers survived. A similar 1860 story of cannibalism came out of Walla Walla, Washington, where the U.S. Army reported rescuing 12 living pioneers and finding 5 dead—who had been keeping the survivors alive by serving as food.

Oregon Trail, 2024. *Courtesy of Jason McLean.*

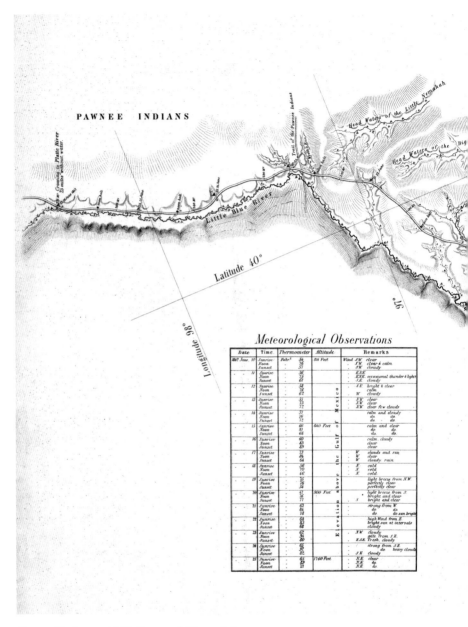

Oregon Trail map, 1846. *Courtesy of Library of Congress.*

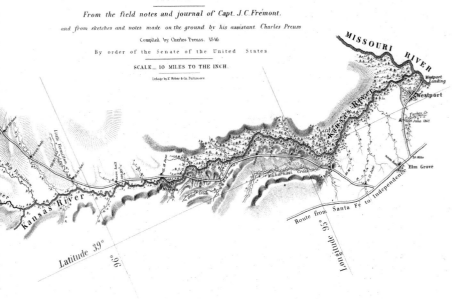

TOPOGRAPHICAL MAP

OF THE

ROAD FROM MISSOURI TO OREGON

COMMENCING AT THE MOUTH OF THE KANSAS IN THE MISSOURI RIVER

AND ENDING AT THE MOUTH OF THE WALLAH-WALLAH IN THE COLUMBIA

In VII Sections

SECTION I

From the field notes and journal of Capt. J.C.Fremont,

and from sketches and notes made on the ground by his assistant Charles Preuss

Compiled by Charles Preuss. 1846

By order of the Senate of the United States

SCALE — 10 MILES TO THE INCH.

Lithogr by E. Weber & Co. Baltimore

REMARKS.

1. The cyphers on the route indicate the distance in miles from Westport Landing.

2. This section abounds with grass, water and fuel so that emigrants may encamp almost anywhere.

3. Elk and Deer, the only game, are very scarce.

As might be expected based on the suffering and deaths along the trail, stories of paranormal energy are plentiful. Some of these stories are based near an old logging camp called Rhododendron Village along the Columbia River Gorge. Specifically, Laurel Hill on the Barlow Road was a terrifying descent for migrants. Wagons had to be lowered with block and tackle, with some ropes tearing, sending wagons hurtling down the hill to a deadly outcome. The alternative of traveling down rapids of the wild Columbia River was no better. This atmosphere of fear and death has spawned sightings of strange glowing orbs, appearing in photographs taken of old bunkhouses. These buildings are said to shake mysteriously when walked through. In one case, an old piano with a mirror on the front was photographed, and a woman's face, unseen in person, appeared in the mirror, as if she was sitting at the piano and playing. A door on the old mess hall where the cook slept is said to open by itself every morning at four o'clock. In 2001, volunteer restoration staff discovered a pair of rock-covered graves, one for a pioneer and the other for a Native. They took photos, and when the film was developed, strange, glowing orbs could be seen hovering above the graves.

Oregon Vortex, Gravity Hill and Other Oddities

America has several so-called mystery spots, at which the laws of science—including gravity—seem to be suspended. These seem to be akin to old circus-type side shows, which tried to attract audiences with bearded ladies, strong men, two-headed goats and other oddities. One such spot in the Pacific Northwest is the Oregon Vortex in southern Oregon's Gold Hill, a roadside attraction that opened in 1930. Legend has it that, before the arrival of White settlers, Natives described the area as a forbidden land, where supernatural forces were at play and through which horses and wildlife refused to walk. It has been described as a spherical force field, half above and half below ground, that acts like a whirlpool of force. It has been reported that brooms balance on end at an angle, back pain disappears, hangovers get worse, balls roll uphill, carpenters' bubble levels malfunction, light rays are bent, optical illusions exist, mass is altered—including the height of visitors fluctuating, depending on where they're standing—and other unexplainable gravitational events occur. Co-located to the Vortex is the House of Mystery, which tilts to one side, at an odd angle, as if through some supernatural cause. Visitors have reported feeling and acting "weird."

The site has been featured on the SyFy network and television programs *Ghost Adventures*, *Supernatural*, and *The X-Files*.

A similar Pacific Northwest mystery spot is called Gravity Hill, fifteen miles north of Prosser in south-central Washington. Those who visit there say that when they put their car in neutral, it begins to roll uphill. Another strange story from Gravity Hill is that if you put powder on the back of your car, a small child's handprints appear as if he or she was pushing your car.

Speaking of oddities, Marsh's Free Museum in Long Beach, Washington, on the Graveyard of the Pacific—we used to live just north of there, in Ocean Park—is a roadside stop displaying numerous oddities. These include a two-headed stuffed goat, other stuffed animals, carnival games of chance—love and strength meters, etc.—the world's largest chopsticks, snakeskins, a shrunken head and most famously the stuffed "Jake the Alligator Man." Jake is described as a "missing link" between reptiles, with the body of a small alligator, and humans, with what appears to be a monkey's head. Most likely Jack is just that, a monkey's head fused to an alligator's body! Marsh's has been displaying oddities since 1921, starting as a candy and ice cream shop, then expanding after the passenger ship *Admiral Benson* ran aground in the fog at nearby Cape Disappointment, mentioned earlier, on February 15, 1930. Marsh's owner, Wellington Marsh Sr., sensed an opportunity to sell to those visiting the area—whether by choice or accident. Marsh's sells other coastal kitschy items and is well worth a stop.

Pirates

In 1693, the Spanish galleon *Santo Cristo de Burgos* wrecked at the base of Oregon's Neahkahnie Mountain, on the state's north coast, just south of present-day Cannon Beach—described earlier. It was sailing from Manila to California, over seven thousand miles, but had gone off course by hundreds of miles due to storms and wrecked. According to Chinook Native oral history, they watched thirty survivors make it to the beach, carrying what was described as a wooden chest in a longboat. Since then, we have surmised the chest contained treasure. The leader—in a large, plumed hat—some modern moviegoers might think of him as a Captain Jack Sparrow–like character from the *Pirates of the Caribbean* movies, and his men dragged the chest onto the mountain, dug a hole and placed the chest in it. Knowing the Chinook feared "malignant spirits" that they believed were released when people die, the captain shot and killed one or more of his crew, throwing

Pirate, 2024. *Courtesy of Jason McLean.*

them on top of the chest. The captain and remaining crew then rowed toward Mexico, and the Natives never dug up the treasure.

Seven years later, in 1700, the wreck of the *Santo Cristo de Burgos* was shoved onto the beach by the megaquake tsunami I described earlier. Out of the ship tumbled chunks of beeswax with strange symbols—it is thought the wax was transported by the Spanish for use in masses in Catholic churches in the new world. However, neither the Natives nor those who found the wax later knew what the symbols meant—with some guessing they were paranormal symbols warning people to stay away from the treasure. I've viewed some samples and believe they were initials and other symbols related to the ship they were on.

The earliest known Euro-American treasure seeker, John Hobson, visited the area in 1843 and learned from the Natives about the captain and his crew burying the treasure chest but never found it. During the late 1800s and into the twentieth century, treasure hunters searched for the treasure on Neahkahnie Mountain. In 1931, Charles Wood and his son Lynn dug a thirty-foot-deep hole into the mountain without adding supports; a cave-in killed them both. Two treasure hunters in 1990 rappelled down Neahkahnie Mountain and entered their inflatable raft to search for the treasure from the water. The men were swept into a cave by waves and stranded there. One of the men, Samuel Logan, was later pulled back out into the ocean by another wave and drowned. It is not clear what became of the other treasure hunter. Dreams of treasure prompted generations of treasure seekers to riddle Neahkahnie Mountain's landscape with pits and trenches, giving it the nickname "mountain of a thousand holes." From 1967 to 1999, the State of Oregon officially allowed treasure hunters to search for treasure on state-owned lands. However, Oregon's "Treasure Trove" statute was repealed in 1999, making treasure hunting illegal on Neahkahnie Mountain and nearby beaches.

An elderly woman on one of my tours described digging for the buried treasure with her parents when she was a little girl. Legend has it that the treasure, still where the Spanish sailors buried it, is guarded by the ghosts of the dead crew and the treasure hunters who died attempting to locate it. The mountain, often shrouded in fog, is the source of many supernatural tales; the 2005 horror movie *The Fog*, which tells of fog bringing vindictive, ghostly mariners who were murdered 134 years prior, was set on a fictional island off the north Oregon coast. The story loosely resembles the real Neahkahnie murders, which occurred over three hundred years earlier and spawned many ghostly tales. The 1985 Steven Spielberg movie *The Goonies* was in part based on this story. Chunks of the ship's wax have continued to be found over the centuries washed ashore, adding to a sense of unexplainable, possibly paranormal events at play, and are on display in the area. In 2022, timbers from the wreck of the *Santo Cristo de Burgos* were located on the Oregon coast.

Satanic Sheriff

This is the strange story of the former chief civil deputy with the Thurston County, Washington's Sheriff's Department—I'm purposely leaving his name out of this story. He was also the chairman of the Thurston County Republican Party. He was tried in 1988 and sentenced to twenty years in prison for rape based on sexually abusing his daughters—his son later accused him of abuse as well. There were stories of Satanic rituals taking place related to the abuse—prosecutors dropped the Satanic portions of the case, including chanting, a high priestess in flowing robes and others wearing Viking-type helmets with horns. There were also stories of babies being slaughtered as part of the rituals. In the legal world, this case is known for the use of recovered-memory therapy (RMT), a much-debated process involving relaxation exercises, age regression, dream interpretation, psychodrama, hypnosis and other means to recover victims' and the accused's repressed memories. The sheriff claimed he was innocent and his confession—based on recovered memory—was coerced; an appeals court disagreed, and he served his sentence before being released in 2003.

A May 16, 1993 *New Yorker* article described family members' testimony as "contradictory" and their memories as having a "hallucinatory" quality. Some compare the conviction with the Salem Witch Trials of 1692 and 1693, which are said to be based on witnesses' false memories of observing acts of witchcraft. This story was the subject of at least one book and a made-for-television movie.

Severed Feet

Severed feet, primarily right feet, started washing ashore along the coasts of northern Washington and southern British Columbia, Canada, in 2007. Nearly two dozen feet have been found, primarily in sneakers, detached from bodies. Some of the shoe brands that have been found include New Balance, Nike and Ozark Trail. In 2007, the first two feet—both right feet—were found in British Columbia just six days apart. The Royal Canadian Mounted Police said that finding them in such a short time frame was suspicious. In 2008, another five feet were found, including in Washington. Speculation about the origins of the feet has ranged from natural disasters, including a 2004 tsunami, to drug dealers, serial killers and human traffickers. Another theory is that at least some of the feet came from a 2005 plane crash off Quadra Island east of Vancouver Island in British Columbia. Five men were on board, but only one of the bodies was found. Others posit that the coast is being used by organized crime as a dumping ground for victims. At least one discovered foot was analyzed by the British Columbia Coroners Service. They couldn't tell how long the foot had been in the water, but the regional coroner said the model of shoe had gone on the market after March 2013. The coroner worked with local police to see if any reported disappearances were connected to the discovery. According to scientists who analyzed the feet, they were likely detached from bodies due to the push and pull of turbulent waves. Further, several of the feet were identified as belonging to individuals who suffered from depression, other forms of mental illness and/or had been reported missing. The King County, Washington Medical Examiner's Office indicated these individuals may have died by suicide by jumping off local bridges into the water; this could explain why a number of corpses have been found floating around these waters.

A detached foot was found in Everett, Washington, on New Year's Day 2019. One doctor speculated ocean scavengers feed on the body but discard the feet, which are bonier, and then the sneaker's buoyancy causes it to float and wash ashore. There are no absolute answers, and the mystery continues. As the coast where these sneakers wash up is in the Graveyard of the Pacific, I usually say to people that the waters are literally a graveyard.

Shanghaiing and Bunko Kelly

It was inexplicably legal to kidnap sailors in America until 1915's Seaman's Act was passed by the U.S. Congress in the face of World War I. This kidnapping was commonly called "shanghaiing," as the kidnappings occurred primarily in the Chinatown sections of cities such as Portland and Astoria, Oregon and Seattle. Another reason was that many of the ships receiving the kidnapped sailors were headed to Shanghai and elsewhere in Asia. The Chinatowns were typically near the waterfront, considered the seedier sides of these cities and home to saloons, brothels and boardinghouses catering

Seattle underground, 2006. *Courtesy of Library of Congress, Carol M. Highsmith, photogra*pher.

to sailors. Another word for this kidnapping was *crimping*, which is thought to refer to either the British term for impressing sailors to unwillingly serve aboard ships or the Dutch word for live fish kept in a tank of water.

Unsuspecting young men were shanghaied from local bars, boardinghouses and even while walking down the sidewalk. Sometimes they were dropped unconscious through trapdoors in the floor, taken through the city's underground tunnels—each of the aforementioned cities' downtowns was raised by as much as two stories, creating undergrounds, due to encroaching waters, sewage, the original downtowns burning down, as discussed earlier, and other reasons—sold as slave labor for fifty dollars a head and forced to serve on ships as sailors in need of crews. There was no escape. There are many paranormal tales of disembodied voices, cold spots, unexplained noises, pushing by unseen hands and other phenomena that are based in these undergrounds. These phenomena are said to be related to the ghosts of shanghaied sailors, kidnapped women—to serve as prostitutes—other crime victims and those who did illegal things there. There are numerous ghost tours through Astoria's, Portland's and Seattle's undergrounds; I've taken several and they are fascinating.

The most infamous shanghaier was Joseph "Bunko" Kelly. He was a British hotelier who, by his own account, crimped some two thousand men and women in the Pacific Northwest over a fifteen-year period, beginning in 1879. He earned his nickname "Bunko" in 1885 after delivering a wooden cigar store Indian as a crew member; the recipient, who paid $50 before knowing what he was receiving, remarked, "This is bunko," or a swindle. He was also called the "Kidnapping King of Portland" and the "Coyote of Portland." As shanghaiing wasn't illegal at the time, Kelly was never arrested for it. However, he was arrested and convicted of murder in 1895 for the killing of G.W. Sayres, an opium smuggler who was hacked to death and thrown into the Willamette River. Kelly was sent to the Oregon State Penitentiary, which was built in 1851, making it the oldest prison in the state. He was inexplicably pardoned by the governor in 1908, based on a petition filed by some of the same people who had worked to have him incarcerated.

Kelly's most infamous crimping reportedly took place in 1893. He was looking for seventeen men to kidnap and provide to the captain of the *Flying Fish*, headed to Shanghai. He passed a Portland, Oregon funeral home and heard multiple men groaning. Kelly found twenty-two seemingly drunken men in the cellar and a keg of deadly embalming fluid from which they had been drinking. He had his men load the twenty-two dying men into carts, then—via the underground tunnels—placed into canoes and finally delivered them to the ship's captain. The captain paid Kelly, only to later discover the twenty-two dead sailors in the ship's hold. The captain had to secure seventeen additional sailors when he reached Astoria. No investigation was ever conducted. Shanghaiing, although practiced elsewhere, was a particularly unique and dreadful part of Pacific Northwest history.

PACIFIC NORTHWEST LEGENDS AND LORE

Ted Bundy

Serial killer Ted Bundy was convicted of murdering two people but claimed to have murdered thirty-eight. He was one of America's most notorious serial killers, and like other serial killers, his story has been featured in books and movies, including 2019's *Extremely Wicked, Shockingly Evil and Vile*.

There are ghost stories based on his actions—I discuss them in *Haunted Puget Sound*. Bundy's study of law and work in law enforcement were antithetical to his murderous actions. He attended the University of Washington in Seattle and then later attended Tacoma's University of Puget Sound's law school. Bundy was inexplicably employed as the assistant director of the Seattle Crime Prevention Advisory Commission. It was around that time that women started disappearing in the Pacific Northwest. One of his victims was Donna Manson, a nineteen-year-old Evergreen State College, Olympia, Washington student who disappeared on March 12, 1974. Bundy admitted to murdering her and "reducing her skull to ash" in his girlfriend's fireplace. There is some dispute on whether he lived in Olympia, but it's believed Bundy worked for the State of Washington there. Further, it's believed he stayed with a friend who attended Evergreen. What is clear is that Bundy lived throughout the Pacific Northwest and committed several of his murders here—Oregon and Washington—with other murders in Colorado, Florida and Utah. He was executed in Florida.

Tumwater State Bank

On September 17, 1981, a bank robber—I'm omitting his name—entered the Tumwater State Bank in Olympia, Washington and fatally shot two female bank tellers. Washington was the last state in the United States with death by hanging; it was allowed until 2018, although the last court-ordered hanging was in 1994. The robber was sentenced to hang for the murders and bank robbery. He appealed his sentence, and a federal judge overturned the death sentence, giving him life in prison instead. The judge ruled hanging would have been "cruel and unusual punishment," but why would a judge find hanging to be cruel and unusual if it was the law of the state? In fact, the judge found the convicted man too obese—at 425 pounds—to hang. The judge said the hanging would have resulted in decapitation, with the murderer's head "popping off." The murderer served his time at the Washington State Penitentiary in Walla Walla until 2006, when he died of liver disease.

Victorian-Era Death Practices

America today is considered a "death-denying" culture, as we don't like to think, talk about or acknowledge death as an inevitable reality. Different cultures have different ways to mark the death of a loved one, friend or acquaintance. Death at home in the care of family, which once was the norm, has in large part been superseded by death in institutions like hospitals, nursing homes and others; although this obviously is not always the case. In 1949, 49.5 percent of deaths occurred in institutions; by 1992, that number had risen to 74 percent—with 20 percent dying at home. Hospice care, focusing on the care, comfort and quality of life of the patient versus just the medical issues, has changed this pattern somewhat. The act of dying away from home has distanced the final stage of life from the rest of living. Further, in our mobile society, we may not be geographically close to the person who died.

The Pacific Northwest, like many parts of America, is full of cemeteries dating to the Victorian era—during the reign of the United Kingdom's Queen Victoria, 1837–1901. One example is Salem, Oregon's Pioneer Cemetery, which was founded in 1854 and is one of the oldest burial grounds in Oregon. The death-related practices of the Victorians of the late nineteenth and early twentieth centuries were very different from our time. It was during this period that necromancy and spiritualism—attempting to communicate with the dead—and the belief in ghosts may have hit their heyday. That was a time haunted by the rapid spread of infectious disease through newly industrialized and crowded cities and towns and the aftermath of the Civil War. Many sought solace through spiritualism and necromancy. Victorians had many superstitions about death that may seem strange to us today. They carried their departed loved ones out of the home feet first so they couldn't look back and call someone else to follow them. They closed curtains and covered mirrors until after the funeral so the deceased's image wouldn't be trapped in the "looking glass." Mirrors and windows seem to have been regarded as paranormal avenues through which the spirits of the dead could travel and become trapped. Victorians observed mourning periods and dressed in mourning—dark and respectful clothes—for weeks, months or years after their loved one's death. They also wore black silk "weeping veils" or caps. After a period, they could wear "half mourning" colors like gray and lavender. Victorians stopped clocks at the time of death to prevent bad luck. They also turned family photographs face down to protect family from possession by the dead. Victorians had photographs

Queen Victoria, 1880. *Courtesy of Library of Congress, New York.*

taken of themselves with their departed loved ones, sometimes having the dead person's body look alive using strings, wires and other mechanisms. They also kept and made mementos from the hair of the dead—these can be found in museums. Theaters were used for public seances, and telling ghost stories was the rage. Finally, as I mentioned earlier, retinal optography was practiced, removing and sharing murder victims' retinas with local photographers for "developing" to see the image of the murderer.

Given the Victorians' strange death practices, it may not be surprising that some of the purportedly most haunted places in the Pacific Northwest are Victorian-era cemeteries. One example is Seattle's Grand Army of the Republic Cemetery, established in 1895, and in which over five hundred Civil War veterans are buried. Full-body apparitions of Civil War soldiers, as well as their cries and wails, have been reported in and around the tombstones for over a century. Next time you pass a cemetery in the Pacific Northwest, especially one from the Victorian era, it is interesting to think about the unique and strange beliefs and practices that were at play.

That completes our discussion of Pacific Northwest aspects of folklore, unrelated to cryptids and curses. I find these stories fascinating, and I hope you do too!

CONCLUSION

In this book, I focused on Pacific Northwest legends and lore. This is the fourth published book I have written that ties in with this genre. In addition to cryptids, legendary curses and folklore, the other substantive area of "dark stories" told in the Pacific Northwest are about ghosts. I don't focus on hauntings in this book but do in three of my other books: *Haunted Graveyard of the Pacific* (2021), *Spirits Along the Columbia River* (2022), and *Haunted Puget Sound* (2024).

From the beginning of time, people have told stories and tales of mysterious and scary experiences, events and creatures. These stories were often a mix of truth, exaggeration, fear, humor and wishful thinking. The more interesting of these stories took on a life of their own, became legends and were passed from one generation to the next. Some stories captured the public's attention by being reported on by newspapers and other media and serving as the focus of investigations, university studies, books, television programs and movies. These are not my stories but rather tales I discovered, researched and am chronicling that have been passed by word of mouth and other means for decades if not centuries. Hopefully I am shedding new light, garnering fresh insights and offering unique interpretations of these tales. I can't, in some cases, corroborate the complete accuracy of these stories but believe they round out the fascinating history of the Pacific Northwest.

As a Pacific Northwest resident, I'm fascinated by the area's history and culture. It was one of the last parts of the United States to be explored and settled, making it seem more wild than other parts of the country. There is

Trees in the mist, 2024. *Courtesy of Jason McLean.*

no better way to discover the beauty and history of the area than to explore the cities, towns and waterways of the area, their history and the folklore—including cryptids and legendary curses that have been shared.

The region is known for great hiking, boating, camping, fishing, biking, clamming, golfing, cranberry cultivation, oyster farming and tourism, while state parks with nineteenth-century military forts and national historic sites welcome history enthusiasts. Bald eagles, black bears, elk, deer and other wildlife call the area home. While the area offers breathtaking, idyllic scenery, it is also considered one of the most supernaturally charged places in the United States. Chilling tales of paranormal phenomena, including cryptids, legendary curses and lore, abound in this northwestern corner of America. There seem to be many ways to get your "chills and thrills" in this part of the country.

The dark skies, strong winds and heavy fog that frequent the Pacific Northwest round out the atmosphere of mystery. The natural and man-made disasters that have struck the area—including earthquakes, fires, tsunamis and volcanoes—and unexplainable events have added a sense of danger and dread. So, if you see someone or something that appears out of place, it may be a cryptid or some other supernatural entity.

I use an evidence-based, investigatory, forensics approach to research and analyze reported legends and lore. I pride myself on my careful research, but in researching these tales, it is clear not everything can be proven beyond a reasonable doubt.

Thank you for joining me as we journeyed around the Pacific Northwest in search of cryptids, legendary curses and lore. I again strongly encourage you to explore the area and visit—of course following all applicable rules and laws, respecting privacy, hours of operation, etc.—the many businesses and landmarks that are open to the public that we've discussed.

BIBLIOGRAPHY

Adams, O. "Species Spotlight: Top 10 Cryptids of the Pacific Northwest." *Cardinal Times*, January 5, 2022. https://cardinaltimes.org.

Ad-lister. "The Most Haunted Items Ever Sold on eBay." https://www.ad-lister.co.uk.

Anderson, J. "Oregon's Haunted Spots." Travel Oregon, September 28, 2016. https://traveloregon.com.

Andress, J. "The Myths and Folklore from Pacific Northwest Contain Some Truly Terrifying Legends." Ranker, June 14, 2019. https://www.ranker.com.

Andrews, E. "10 Little-Known Facts About the Lewis and Clark Expedition." October 26, 2015. https://www.history.com.

Answers with Joe. "They Thought It Was Hail. It Was Something Way Weirder." December 12, 2022. https://answerswithjoe.com.

Aramark Nation's Vacation. "The Spooky History of Crater Lake: Crater Lake's Spookiest Stories." thenationsvacation.com.

Astonishing Legends. "The Stick Indians." November 25, 2018. https://astonishinglegends.com.

Ausler, N. "8 Ways to Break a Curse or Hex." November 27, 2022. https://www.yourtango.com.

Baker, M. "FBI Has Chased Hundreds of D.B. Cooper Ghosts." KOMO News, Associated Press, August 4, 2011.

Barratt, K. "Understanding Tuunbaq and What It Represents in the Terror." Out of Lives, January 6, 2021. https://www.outoflives.net.

Battistella, M. "Oregon Vortex (House of Mystery)." *Oregon Encyclopedia*, June 1, 2022. https://oregonencyclopedia.org.

Beach Connection. "What Ghosts Gather Around Fort Stevens." https://www.beachconnection.net.

Belyk, R.C. *Great Shipwrecks of the Pacific Coast*. New York: Wiley, 2001.

Benjamin, R. "Cryptozoology—The Evidence of Creatures Whose Existence Is Uncertain." Biology Online, October 7, 2020. https://www.biologyonline.com.

Bennett-Smith, M. "Vampire Graveyard Unearthed in Poland." *Huffington Post*, July 12, 2013. https://www.huffpost.com.

Benoit, M. "The History Behind the Bellingham 'Curse.'" Whatcom Talk. https://www.whatcomtalk.com.

Bhattacharjee, S. "7 Most Common Superstitions of Seafarers." Marine Insight, August 26, 2021. https://www.marineinsight.com.

Blalock, B. *The Oregon Shanghaiers: Columbia River Crimping from Astoria to Portland*. Charleston, SC: The History Press, 2014.

Bloom, L. "10 Most Haunted States in America (You Won't Believe the Scariest)." Forbes, October 26, 2020. https://www.forbes.com.

Blumberg, J. "A Brief History of the Salem Witch Trials." *Smithsonian Magazine*, October 24, 2022.

Board, W. "One Legend Found, Many Still to Go." *New York Times*, October 2, 2005.

BookBrowse. "Overcoming Arkoudaphobia: The Rarity of Bear Attacks in North America." https://www.bookbrowse.com.

A Book of Creatures. "Amhuluk." https://abookofcreatures.com.

Bousfield, E.L., and P.H. LeBlond. "An Account of *Cadborosaurus Willsi*, New Genus, New Species, A Large Aquatic Reptile from the Pacific Coast of North America." *Amphipacifica* 1, suppl. 1 (1995): 3–25. https://cryptozoologicalreferencelibrary.wordpress.com/b/.

Brandman, M., and T. Potter. "Sacagawea (c. 1788–C. 1812/1884?)." National Women's History Museum, https://www.womenshistory.org.

Brandt, A. "Sex, Dog Meat, and the Lash: Odd Facts About Lewis and Clark." *National Geographic*, December 7, 2003. https://www.nationalgeographic.com.

Brenner, K. "Folklore & Nature: Cadborosaurus." October 23, 2019. https://www.metrofieldguide.com.

Brode, N. "U.S. Belief in Sasquatch Has Risen Since 2020." Civic Science, August 2, 2022. https://civicscience.com.

Browning, T., dir. *Dracula*. Universal Pictures. 1931.

Campuzano, E. "Oregon Ghost Stories: 31 Famous Haunted Places." Oregonlive, October 22, 2016. https://www.oregonlive.com.

Cardakli, B. "Washington State Cryptids You've Never Heard Of." Her Campus, March 9, 2023. https://www.hercampus.com.

Carey, B. "Gigantic Apes Coexisted with Early Humans, Study Finds" Live Science, November 7, 2005. https://www.livescience.com.

Cartwright, M. "Pirate Punishments in the Golden Age of Piracy." World History Encyclopedia, October 7, 2021. https://www.worldhistory.org.

CBS News. "Alleged D.B. Cooper DNA Not a Match." August 8, 2011. https://www.cbsnews.com.

———. "Bigfoot Sighter Sticks By Story." July 10, 2000. https://www.cbsnews.com.

Cellania, M. "7 Fugitives Who Became Folk Heroes." Mental Floss, July 20, 2010. https://www.mentalfloss.com.

———. "10 Legendary Monsters of North America: Part One." Mental Floss, October 25, 2012. https://www.mentalfloss.com.

———. "10 Legendary Monsters of North America: Part Two." Mental Floss, November 1, 2012. https://www.mentalfloss.com.

Center for the Study of the Pacific Northwest. "The Changing World of the Pacific Northwest Indians." University of Washington, https://www.washington.edu.

Cep, C. "Why Did So Many Victorians Try to Speak with The Dead?" *New Yorker*, May 24, 2021.

Cobb, T. *Ghosts of Portland, Oregon.* Atglen, PA: Schiffer Publishing, 2007.

Conradt, S. "7 of History's Strangest Mass Hysteria Events—The Seattle Windshield Pitting Delusion." Mental Floss, June 12, 2023. https://www.mentalfloss.com.

Coogan, S. Seattle. "Portland Rank High on List of Top US Cities for Vampires." KIRO 7 News, October 29, 2023. https://www.kiro7.com.

Cox, W.T. *Fearsome Creatures of the Lumberwoods: With a Few Desert and Mountain Beasts.* Whitefish, MT: Kessinger Publishing, 2010.

Crair, B. "Why Do So Many People Still Want to Believe in Bigfoot?" *Smithsonian Magazine*, September 2018.

Crime + Investigation. "6 Terrifying Facts about Gary Ridgway 'The Green River Killer.'" https://www.crimeandinvestigation.co.uk.

Cryptids and Myths Wiki. "List of Cryptozoological Bears." https://allcryptid.fandom.com.

Cryptid Wiki. "Cactus Cat." https://cryptidz.fandom.com.

———. "Gumberoo." https://cryptidz.fandom.com.

Daily Mail. "The Tough Men of Timber." December 15, 2015. https://www.dailymail.co.uk.

Dalton, A. *The Graveyard of the Pacific: Shipwreck Tales from the Depths of History.* Victoria, BC: Heritage House Publishing, 2020.

Davis, B.W. "The Curse of Chief Seattle." *Postmodern Urban Human,* January 17, 2016. http://postmodernurbanhuman.blogspot.com.

Davis, J. *Haunted Tour of the Pacific Northwest.* St. Anthony, NL: Norseman Ventures, 2001.

Davis, J., and Eufrasio, A. *Weird Washington: Your Travel Guide to Washington's Local Legends and Best Kept Secrets.* New York: Sterling, 2008.

Denova, R. "Ten Plagues of Egypt." World History Encyclopedia, February 18, 2022. https://www.worldhistory.org.

Deur, G., and C. La Follette. *The Mountain of a Thousand Holes: Shipwreck Traditions and Treasure Hunting on Oregon's North Coast.* Portland State University study, 2018.

Discovery. "What Were the Oakville Blobs and What Caused Them?" May 17, 2022. https://www.discoveryuk.com/.

Doro, B. "15 Chilling Folktales, Traditions, and Objects from Around the World." *In Good Taste,* October 9, 2018. https://www.invaluable.com.

Downer, D.L. *Classic American Ghost Stories: 200 Years of Ghost Lore from the Great Plains, New England, the South and the Pacific Northwest.* Atlanta: August House Publishers, 1990.

Drawson, M.C. *Treasures of the Oregon Country.* Salem, OR: Dee Publishing Company, 1975.

Duncan-Strong, W. *The Occurrence and Wider Implications of a "Ghost Cult" on the Columbia River Suggested by Carvings in Wood, Bone and Stone.* Whitefish, MT: Literary Licensing, 2013.

Dunkelberger, S. "The Country's Worst Street Accident Took Place in Tacoma." SouthSound Talk, January 17, 2017. https://www.southsoundtalk.com.

Duwamish Tribe. "Chief Si'ahl." https://www.duwamishtribe.org.

Dwyer, J. *Ghost Hunter's Guide to Portland and the Oregon Coast.* Gretna, LA: Pelican Publishing Company, 2015.

Education World. "Oregon Trail." https://www.educationworld.com.

Ellis, R. *Singing Whales and Flying Squid: The Discovery of Marine Life.* Lanham, MD: Lyons Press, 2006.

Erdelac, E. *Monstrumfuhrer.* N.p.: Comet Press, 2017.

Evans, Z. "Top Five Mythical Birds in Legend and Folklore." Folklore Thursday, January 23, 2020. https://folklorethursday.com.

Field, M.J., and C.K. Cassel, eds. "A Profile of Death and Dying in America." In *Approaching Death: Improving Care at the End of Life*, chapter 2. Washington, D.C.: National Academies Press, 1992. https://www.ncbi.nlm.nih.gov/books/NBK233601/.

Finkbeiner, A. "The Great Quake and the Great Drowning." *Slate*, September 15, 2015. https://slate.com.

Finn, J. "'Colossal Claude,' The Great Columbia Sea Serpent." *Offbeat Oregon*, February 4, 2020. https://www.thenewsguard.com.

Fox, A. "This Hotel Is the Most Haunted in America." Travel + Leisure, October 7, 2022. https://www.travelandleisure.com.

Franhao, D., and D. Olson. "Demonic Influence: The Negative Mental Health Effects of Belief in Demons." *Journal for the Scientific Study of Religion* 55, no. 3 (September 2016): 498–515. https://www.jstor.org.

Fritscher, L. "Understanding the Fear of Cats." Very Well Mind, February 17, 2022. https://www.verywellmind.com.

Funeral Basics. "8 Intriguing Funeral Customs from the Victorian Era." https://www.funeralbasics.org.

Gabriel, B. "What Obstacles Did Lewis and Clark's Expedition Encounter?" Classroom, June 25, 2018. https://classroom.synonym.com.

Gendron, J. "History of Sasquatch in Washington May Surprise Some." *Spokesman-Review*, August 3, 2023.

———. "Tacoma Deemed Hot-Spot for Bigfoot Sightings in WA. A Law Protects Hunters from Killing It." *News Tribune*, May 9, 2023.

Gentling, D. *The Bandage Man Legend: A Cannon Beach Legend*. University of Oregon's Northwest Folklore program, 1974.

Gibbs, J.A. *Pacific Graveyard*. Portland, OR: Binford & Mort Publishing, 1991.

———. *Peril at Sea*. Atglen, PA: Schiffer Publishing Ltd., 1997.

Goings, A. *The Port of Missing Men: Billy Gohl, Labor, and Brutal Times in the Pacific Northwest*. Seattle: University of Washington Press, 2020.

Goodwin, C. "Strange, Panther-Like Creature Prowls the Gorge." CCC News-Columbia Community Connection. https://columbiacommunityconnection.com.

Greenman, M. "Haunted Harbor: A Ghost Hunter's Guide to Haunted Places in Grays Harbor County." Grays Harbor Talk. https://www.graysharbortalk.com.

Grimm, D. "The Legendary Dire Wolf May Not Have Been a Wolf at All." *Science*, January 13, 2021. https://www.science.org.

Guiley, R.E. "Ghost of a Suicide at Haunted North Head Lighthouse." Visionary Living Inc., May 24, 2016. https://www.visionaryliving.com.

Guzman, J. "Doctor Explains Why 21 Human Feet in Sneakers Washed on Shore." The Hill, August 23, 2021. https://thehill.com.

Hanover, D. "Seafaring Superstitions & Marine Myth Rituals Explained." Dive Training, August 6, 2006. https://dtmag.com.

Heidelberg, A. "The Oregon Trail Legacy Is Even Darker Than We Realized." History Collection, February 14, 2023. https://historycollection.com.

Hirschfelder, A., and P. Molin. The Encyclopedia of Native American Religions. New York: Facts on File, 1992.

History. "Kenneth Arnold." February 22, 2010. https://www.history.com.

Hoad, P. "How the Predator Franchise Is Breaking New Ground for Native Americans on Screen." Guardian, July 29, 2022. https://www.theguardian.com.

HowStuffWorks. "9 Legends of American Folklore." https://people.howstuffworks.com.

Johnston, R.D., and D. Brinkley. The Making of America: The History of the United States from 1492 to the Present. National Geographic Children's Books, 2002.

Judd, R. "Next Generations Tell the Buried Tales of Chinese Northwesterners." Seattle Times, June 21, 2013.

Kashino, M. "I Spent the Night in a Haunted Asylum and I Still Can't Explain What I Saw." Washingtonian, October 25, 2018.

Kasischke, L. "Playground Tales: Fifteen Horror Stories My Classmates Told Me." HuffPost, April 17, 2013. https://www.huffpost.com.

Kavin, K. "7 Most Haunted Lighthouses in the United States." Boatsaver, October 4, 2022. https://www.boatsetter.com.

Kent, L. "The 10 Most Convincing Bigfoot Sightings." Outside, March 10, 2023. https://www.outsideonline.com.

KHQ News. "Bigfoot Sighting? WSDOT Cameras Capture Sasquatch-Like Creature on Sherman, Snoqualmie Passes." January 23, 2020. https://www.khq.com.

Kirsch, J. "Police: Lincoln County Man Killed Mom with Stake Because He Believed She Was a Vampire." KATU-ABC-2, March 14, 2024. https://kpic.com.

Kozik, J. Shipwrecks of the Pacific Northwest: Tragedies and Legacies of a Perilous Coast. Guilford, CT: Globe Pequot Press, 2020.

Ladd, K., B. Macaluso, and A. Schubak. "37 Things Americans Do That Confuse the Rest of the World." Yahoo, June 25, 2018. https://www.yahoo.com.

Langston, K. "The 10 Best Bigfoot Movies Ranked." Screen Rant, April 10, 2023. https://screenrant.com.

Larkin, B. "The 30 Most Fascinating Unsolved Mysteries in America." Best Life, March 13, 2018. https://bestlifeonline.com.

Lee, R. "1947: Year of the Flying Saucer." Smithsonian, June 24, 2022. https://airandspace.si.edu.

Legends of America. "Monsters and Sea Serpents." https://www.legendsofamerica.com.

———. "Navajo Skinwalkers—Witches of the Southwest." https://www.legendsofamerica.com.

"Lewis and Clark: The Journey Ends." *Smithsonian* magazine, December 2005. https://www.smithsonianmag.com.

Little, B. "6 Famous Curses and Their Origins." History, October 19, 2020. https://www.history.com.

Loebenberg, P. "Show to Feature Tale of Maryland Monster." CBS News, February 27, 2014. https://www.cbsnews.com/.

Logan, D. "The Air Force Apparently Once Classified Bigfoot as a 'Dangerous Animal.'" Exemplore News, February 9, 2023. https://exemplore.com/news/air-force-bigfoot.

Mangan, D. "He Got the FBI to Test 'Bigfoot' Hair in the 1970s—And This 93-Year-Old Man Is Still Searching for Sasquatch." CNBC, June 5, 2019. https://www.cnbc.com.

McConaghy, L. "Charles Mitchell, Slavery, and Washington Territory in 1860." Black Past, July 14, 2012. https://www.blackpast.org.

McCormack, J.W. "Hitler Used Werewolves, Vampires, and Astrology to Brainwash Germany." Vice, June 29, 2017. https://www.vice.com.

Mitchell, R. "7 Legendary Cryptids That Turned Out to Be Real!" Ancient Origins, October 12, 2022. https://www.ancient-origins.net.

Mohsin, M. "Legend of the Black-eyed Children." Business Standard, March 13, 2020. https://www.tbsnews.net.

Moncrease, B. "A Curse More Than a Half-Century Old with Binghamton Ties." Spectrum News, October 28, 2016. https://spectrumlocalnews.com.

Montero, J. "A Leading Sasquatch Researcher Is Opening Oregon's First Bigfoot Museum." Willamette Week, July 31, 2019. https://www.wweek.com.

Morton, C. "The 32 Most Haunted Places in America." Condé Nast Traveler, October 7, 2021. https://www.cntraveler.com.

Mother Nature. "Black Cats: Myths, Legends, and Superstitions." October 31, 2022. https://mother-nature.ca.

My Mondo Trading. "The Native Meaning of…Symbology, Myths and Legends." https://www.mymondotrading.com.

Napoli, D. "Cats Rule in Ancient Egypt." National Geographic Kids. https://kids.nationalgeographic.com.

National Park Service. "Death and Danger on the Emigrant Trails." December 29, 2020. https://www.nps.gov.

Neuharth, S. "Is Bigfoot Dangerous?" MeatEater, September 16, 2020. https://www.themeateater.com.

Nour, S. "The First 10 Horror Films in Recorded History." Reel Rundown, March 7, 2023. https://reelrundown.com.

Orcasonian. "When Orcas Island Had a Sea Serpent." September 25, 2021. https://theorcasonian.com.

Oregon Journal. "Bunko Kelly Pardoned After Thirteen Years." July 21, 1907.

Oxley, D. "Did You Know?: Why You Shouldn't Mess with Bigfoot in Washington State." KUOW—NPR Network, December 8, 2022. https://www.kuow.org.

Pagliarulo, A. "Why Paganism and Witchcraft Are Making a Comeback." NBC News, October 30, 2022. https://www.nbcnews.com.

Paradis, E.C. "Spiritual Meanings of Black Birds: Uncovering the Sacred Symbology." Impeccable Nest. https://www.linkedin.com/posts.

Perry, D. "How a 1924 Bigfoot Battle on Mt. St. Helens Helped Launch a Legend: Thowback Thursday." *Oregonian*, January 25, 2018. https://www.oregonlive.com.

Pester, P. "Bigfoot? Sasquatch? Nope, It's Probably Just a Black-Bear—Unless You Live in Florida." Live Science, January 24, 2024. https://www.livescience.com.

Philipo. "The Chinese Deadline." blipfoto. https://www.blipfoto.com.

Phillips, T. "More Animal Symbolism: Eagle Symbolism." Pure Spirit. http://www.pure-spirit.com.

Pursiful, D. "Vampire Vednesdays: Mosquito Folk." *Into the Wonder*, October 23, 2019. https://intothewonder.wordpress.com.

Ramirez, R. "Secrets of the Horror Genre." Story Grid, 2018. https://storygrid.com.

Redfern, N. *The Bigfoot Book: The Encyclopedia of Sasquatch, Yeti and Cryptid Primates.* Canton Carter Township, MI: Visible Ink Press, 2015.

Rimpoche, Tsim. "10 Weird Facts about Bigfoot." January 27, 2016. https://www.tsemrinpoche.com.

Rough Guides. "Weird America: 9 of the USA's Most Bizarre Traditions." April 1, 2020. https://www.roughguides.com.

Schild, D., and A. Wang. "20 Urban Legends Americans Can't Stop Talking About." Business Insider, September 27, 2019. https://www.businessinsider.com.

Schmidt, S. "15 Urban Legends We Want to See in Supernatural." Screen Rant, October 17, 2016. https://screenrant.com.

Seattle Terrors. "Grand Army of the Republic Cemetery." https://seattleterrors.com.

Shuker, K. "Caterpillar Bears, Bulldog Bears, and God Bears-Ursine Cryptids of Kamchatka." shukernature, September 7, 2014. https://karlshuker.blogspot.com.

16% Nation. "The Mysterious Kushtaka: A Cryptid of the Pacific Northwest" January 22, 2023. https://16nation.com.

Speakman, K. "New Evidence Discovered in D.B. Cooper Skyjacking Case Uncovers 'a Compelling Person of Interest.'" People, January 14, 2024. https://people.com.

Stoker, B. Dracula. Edinburgh: Archibald Constable and Company, 1897.

Strauss, B. "The Real Story Behind Dinosaurs and Dragons." ThoughtCo., October 10, 2019. https://www.thoughtco.com.

Summers, K. "Investigating the Murderous Ghost of William Gohl, the Ghoul of Grays Harbor." Week in Weird, February 2, 2015. http://weekinweird.com/2015/02/02/ghosts-ghoul-grays-harbor/.

Tabit, J. "7 Cursed Objects Around the World Guaranteed to Ruin Your Life." Fodors Travel, May 18, 2020. https://www.fodors.com/news/photos/7-cursed-objects-around-the-world-guaranteed-to-ruin-your-life.

Taylor, T. "The Arizona Thunderbird." Weird U.S. http://www.weirdus.com.

Thrillist. "The Creepiest Place to Visit in Every State." October 5, 2022. https://www.thrillist.com.

Tikkanen, A. "Why Are People Afraid of Clowns?" Britannica. https://www.britannica.com.

Travel Channel. "The Lewis and Clark Conspiracy." Lost Secrets, Season 1, Episode 5. https://www.travelchannel.com.

Triezenberg, J. "The North Coast's Legendary Sea Monsters." Astorian, October 9, 2020. https://www.dailyastorian.com.

Trucker, A. "Meriwether Lewis' Mysterious Death." Smithsonian magazine, October 2009. https://www.smithsonianmag.com.

Tryon, H.H. Fearsome Critters. Cornwall, NY: Idlewild Press, 1939.

University of Washington. "Pacific Northwest Reference Collection: Northwest Native Americans." https://guides.lib.uw.edu.

U.S. Department of Veterans Affairs. "Celebrating America's Freedoms: The American Bald Eagle." https://www.va.gov.

Walkter, Z. "The Hope Diamond: 13 Victims of The Hope Diamond Curse." DoYouRemember? https://doyouremember.com.

Wang, KY. "Severed Feet—Still Inside Shoes—Keep Mysteriously Washing Up on Pacific Northwest Shores." *Washington Post*, February 11, 2016. https://www.washingtonpost.com.

Wood, M. "The Most Haunted Hotels in the World." *USA Today*, October 30, 2014. https://www.usatoday.com.

Wright, E.W. *Lewis & Dryden's Maritime History of the Pacific Northwest*. Portland, OR: Lewis & Dryden Printing Co., 1895.

Wright, L. "Remembering Satan—Part II: What Was Going On in Thurston County?" *New Yorker*, May 16, 1993. https://www.newyorker.com.

Yater, G. "John Colter Biography." Lewis and Clark Trail Heritage Foundation, May 1992. https://lewisandclarkinkentucky.org.

You & Meow. "A Feline Mystery: Why Cats Are So Deeply Associated with Spirituality." August 14, 2018. https://www.youandmeow.co.uk.

Yuko, E. "The Terrifying Rise of Haunted Tourism." Bloomberg, October 28, 2021. https://www.bloomberg.com.

Zapato, L. "Tree Octopi." Boston University, March 8, 1998. https://www.bu.edu.

ABOUT THE AUTHOR

Photo by David J. Kitmacher.

Ira Wesley Kitmacher is a historian and published author of books on American— *Haunted Graveyard of the Pacific, Spirits Along the Columbia River, Haunted Puget Sound* and *Pacific Northwest Legends and Lore,* and European— *Monsters and Miracles: Horror, Heroes and the Holocaust,* history and folklore. His books have appeared on Amazon's best-seller lists and are available through most booksellers. Arcadia Publishing has adapted two of Ira's books for school-age readers: *The Ghostly Tales of the Pacific Northwest* and *The Ghostly Tales of Puget Sound.*

Ira has appeared in television news programs, filmed documentaries, magazines, radio programs, podcasts, newspapers, museum events and conferences. He is a professor, teaching graduate-level courses at Georgetown University in Washington, D.C., and Portland State University in Oregon, as well as undergraduate courses at other colleges. He has taught college classes based on his books.

Ira is an experienced and acclaimed speaker and guide, serving as an onboard historian and destination speaker for a major cruise ship line and conducting tours based on his books. He is a retired senior U.S. government executive as well as a licensed attorney; is currently working as a consultant, legal expert witness and commissioner on a Pacific Northwest Historic Commission; and is a member of the Historical Writers Association. Ira holds Juris Doctor (JD), Master of Science and Bachelor of Arts degrees. He is a graduate of Harvard University and other senior executive leadership programs.

Ira has a passion for history and folklore.

ALSO BY IRA WESLEY KITMACHER

Haunted Graveyard of the Pacific
Haunted Puget Sound
Monsters and Miracles: Horror, Heroes and the Holocaust
Pacific Northwest Legends and Lore
Solomon's Steps
Spirits Along the Columbia River

FOR YOUNG READERS

The Ghostly Tales of Puget Sound
The Ghostly Tales of the Pacific Northwest

Visit us at
www.historypress.com